ALTAR, GIFT AND GOSPEL

ALTAR,
GIFT AND GOSPEL

53 Meditations on certain
Gospel Passages

by
GIUSEPPE DE LUCA

TEMPLEGATE
Publishers
SPRINGFIELD, ILLINOIS

Library of Congress Catalog Card Number 67:21048

From the original Italian *Commenti al Vangelo Quotidiano*
published by Morcelliana, Brescia

Translated by Dorothy White

NIHIL OBSTAT: E. Hardwick, *Censor Deputatus*

IMPRIMATUR: + Charles Grant, *Vic. Cap.*

Northantoniae, die 7a martii 1967.

The *Nihil Obstat* and *Imprimatur* are a declaration that a book or
pamphlet is considered to be free from doctrinal or moral error. It is not
implied that those who have granted the *Nihil Obstat* and *Imprimatur*
agree with the contents, opinions or statements expressed.

Printed in Great Britain

To Mgr Giuseppe De Luca
my uncle according to the flesh,
my father in the priesthood,
in the 86th year of his age,
and 61st year of his priesthood.

Introduction

by

ARCHBISHOP H. E. CARDINALE

Apostolic Delegate to Great Britain

It is no easy task to introduce the author of this book in an appropriate manner to the non-Italian reader. It is even more difficult for me, who knew Don Giuseppe De Luca too well to be able to contain his colourful personality in one quick glance. Another book would be required to give an adequate account of his overwhelming activity as a writer, a bibliophile and especially as a priest. I do hope that some day he will have an official biographer. Here I shall attempt to trace only a very brief sketch of his versatile personality and achievements.

Don Giuseppe did not live to longevity. He was born in 1898 and died at 64 after a busy and varied career, at the peak of his productiveness, when so much was being expected from what he himself was still expecting to accomplish. At his death-bed, shortly before he passed away on the feast of his heavenly patron, St Joseph, stood his earthly patron, another Joseph, who had chosen for himself the name of John XXIII, speaking words of encouragement. Both reared to the priesthood at the Roman Seminary, their acquaintance had sprung from an almost casual meeting in 1945 when Archbishop Roncalli was Papal Nuncio to France. It was renewed and strengthened at Venice in 1955 and continued

7

at the Vatican, becoming one of those few friendships so close to Pope John's heart. From a common love for historical and biblical studies it developed into an intimate harmony of souls, which afforded Don Giuseppe great consolation in the last years of his life.

And what a busy life was his! To appreciate its rhythm one would have to be acquainted with the history of the Roman scene during the agitated period spanning over half a century, from the condemnation of Modernism through two world wars, with Fascism in between, to the Second Vatican Council. There was hardly an aspect or an item of that stirring time which did not intrigue Don Giuseppe, and somehow involve him. His opinion was often sought, but he never pressed himself to the fore.

His main concern was in his studies. Though his love for learning knew no bounds, he concentrated chiefly on literature, philosophy, history, art and apologetics. His writings— books, lectures and sermons—dating from 1923 to 1962 are an imposing conspectus of his tireless work of research and criticism in many fields. His critical spirit made him uncompromising and bluntly outspoken. But his sting was tempered by his charming bonhomie and unfailing humour, which made him very popular but did not always protect him against resentment. The consequent misunderstandings were a cause of deep suffering to him, whose heart harboured charity for all and malice for none.

Don Giuseppe was a great admirer of the eminent figures of English Catholicism, which he endeavoured to introduce to the Italian world, through his *English Miscellany*. He was especially attracted by such giants as St Thomas More, Cardinal Pole, Gerard Manley Hopkins, Cardinal Newman, Hilaire Belloc and Gilbert K. Chesterton. While working in the Roman Curia he developed a keen interest in the question of Anglican Orders, and had access to the pertinent Vatican documents. Till the very end he hoped to edit the preliminary drafts of Leo XIII's *Epistula ad Anglos,* as Cardinal Tardini had edited those of the Rerum Novarum.

His hobby was to collect books, and to read them from

cover to cover. No private library could contend with his collection in number and value. He died penniless: all his fortune was in his books. But his studies did not isolate him from the world outside. His range of friendships comprised a long list of famous contemporaries, whose faithful confidant he was. His social contacts, which included men like the Italian Communist leader Togliatti, were directed at bringing Christ into the lives of the great of this world. But over and above his many-sided interests were the joy of his priesthood and his love for the Church. He never bore the burden of a parish, but he dedicated himself generously to the apostolate among the old, spending two hours a day in the homes of the Little Sisters of the Poor, visiting, consoling and entertaining the inmates with Christlike charity and gentleness. He was known to all as 'Don Giuseppe', though he was invested with the dignity of a Domestic Prelate. His sermons on the Gospel and the spiritual life, many of which were broadcast by radio, clearly reveal what his companionship with the word of God and the motions of the Spirit meant to him.

One is impressed by the striking resemblance of mind and character this fine Italian priest bore, on the whole, to Monsignor Ronald Knox.

As they did in his English contemporary, sanctity and genius, piety and scholarship, wit and compassion went together in this warm and very human being, who was a rich ornament to the Church and to the world of learning. He died on the battlefield, as he had hoped, his last energies reduced by fatigue, but his spirits as high as could be, after a short but very trying and painful illness. His last words were: 'Come, Lord Jesus, delay no longer!' This ejaculation, which had been the longing of his whole life, became the jubilant salutation with which he greeted his Maker and Saviour, who had come to free him from his tribulations. This cry is echoed throughout his spiritual writings.

In *Commento al Vangelo Quotidiano* Monsignor Giuseppe De Luca shows himself to be above all a man of deep prayer, who sets out to teach others the ways of God only after having himself suffered and passed through the inspiring experiences of the spiritual life.

This manual of short meditations on Gospel passages will fascinate the reader who will easily understand why it was Pope John's favourite bedside book till the very end.

5th December, 1966

I

'And when you fast, do not look dismal, like the hypocrites, for they disfigure their faces that their fasting may be seen by men. Truly, I say to you, they have their reward. But whenever you fast, anoint your head and wash your face, that your fasting may not be seen by men but by your Father who is in secret; and your Father who sees in secret will reward you.'

Matthew vi, 16–18

'Your Father sees in secret'

Once upon a time Christians practised virtue 'in secret', in a hidden life, detached from this world; their virtue was robust, it was born of intimacy with the divine, and was full of shy reserve. Just because men really loved our Father in Heaven they felt an unwillingness, almost a horror, at the thought of offering him what had already been offered to their own pride or to the curiosity of the world. Who would wish to present a flower from another's faded bouquet? Who would place before his friend a dish that we or others had already rejected? Who would make a present of some sweet titbit already nibbled and tasted, or of a choice wine already sipped? It seems inconceivable, but this is just what we regularly do when we make an offering to the poor, or to God: we offer something we no longer care about, something we would otherwise cast aside—like a squeezed orange.

11

Let us reflect a little. The created world is immense, extended in immeasurable space and the terrifying vastness of time, immense in the multiplicity of its most delicate and minute details. A flower petal, a shaft of light, the sound of a distant waterfall, a puff of wind—are the signs of the wealth and variety of a life which, for the most part, is quite beyond our reach. Let us imagine the life of all creation, in its infinity and secrecy, and reflect that this life unfolds itself before God and for his glory, although we ourselves understand so little of it. Whatever part of it comes into our own hands we seize upon and twist away from its first and final destination, because we want it to belong to us, and be for our own glory.

And all that springs up within us, in our innermost being, must be entirely ours, for us alone; we even keep for ourselves the best part of what we do for God. We use not only our virtuous acts but even our prayers to our Father as a means of flattering our vanity, for we want others to hear and to tell us how good and clever and holy we are.

We are in a bad way, sinful and unsatisfactory Christians that we are. Silence makes us insipid, cowardly, inept. Only noise can stimulate us, but it dissipates our powers. When we are told to recollect ourselves in tranquillity we rot like stagnant water; when we are stirred to action we lose sight of God and become just like the world which God condemns. At the beginning of Lent, we should try to rediscover that life 'in secret', which is so humble and yet so sacred, which in its beauty seems a thing from Heaven and in its modesty is within the reach of all—the hidden prayer, the hidden sorrow, even the hidden deed.

'Your Father,' said Jesus, 'sees in secret.' He does not see by our light, but by his own, and his light is our darkness.

2

'As he entered Capernaum a centurion came forward to him, beseeching him and saying, "Lord, my servant is lying paralysed at home, in terrible distress," and he said to him, "I will come and heal him." But the centurion answered him, "Lord, I am not worthy to have you come under my roof; but only say the word, and my servant will be healed. For I am a man under authority with soldiers under me; and I say to one, 'Go,' and he goes, and to another, 'Come,' and he comes, and to my slave, 'Do this,' and he does it." When Jesus heard him he marvelled, and said to those who followed him, "Truly, I say to you, not even in Israel have I found such faith...." And to the centurion Jesus said, "Go; be it done for you as you have believed." And the servant was healed at that very moment.'

Matthew viii, 5–13

'Be it done for you as you have believed'

This answer which our Lord gave to the centurion is not intended for him alone, in his particular case—it is the answer for us all, and for every case. It is, one might say, a law, and one of those laws that permit of fewest exceptions. The measure of what we receive in the way of salvation and grace is the actual measure of our faith. We believe little, and receive little; we believe much and receive much; we believe nothing and we are nothing and have no part in the divine

13

life. Faith is not so much the gate of salvation, opened once and for ever, as the gate which swings open to every saving act, every extraordinary grace. It is true that faith must not be understood in the popular sense, as a sort of auto-suggestion, or a spell which we bind upon ourselves, nor is it perhaps to be understood in the strict sense of mental assent resting on divine authority. In many passages in the Gospels and other New Testament books, faith seems to be the same as love: it is the beginning and also the final end of love. To believe means to trust, to draw near, to know, to commit oneself entirely; so it means giving oneself, that is, loving.

When we consider our wretched lives we see that we usually love the things which do not satisfy, cannot satisfy, our love. Our love is such that it can find its true and only fulfilment nowhere but in God; what use are creatures to us, or rather, what use is this or that creature? The will, like the intelligence, is essentially a spiritual force which can never find sufficient scope in material things. When we add grace to thought and love, that is, an element of the divine life to elements of nature, we shall begin to know what we really are. Or better, what we ought to be, and could be. Instead, we live like vermin, crazed, blind and filthy.

Our faith can move mountains; here is an expression which astonishes only those who do not realize the meaning of what they say, or hear others say. In fact, what is the moving of a mountain compared with the re-birth of a soul from sin? or forgiveness freely bestowed? or kindness shown to an enemy? or words of resignation uttered by a man dying in pain? Must we always pay more attention to what is visible, audible, tangible? Can we never begin to understand the height, depth and breadth of spiritual things?

Is the example of Jesus and the saints not enough to convince us that, if we really had faith, physical forces and material things would scatter like dust before a puff of wind? We are like people who live near a waterfall, and never get used to its noise, but spend all their days and all their lives listening to the thunder of the falling water, never speaking, or wishing to hear spoken, about anything else.

The noise of the world deafens us, and if our ears are closed how will faith make itself heard?

'Faith comes from what is heard'[1]

1. Rom. x, 17.

3

'You have heard that it was said: "You shall love your neigh-bour and hate your enemy." But I say to you, Love your ene-mies and pray for those who persecute you, so that you may be sons of your Father who is in heaven; for he makes his sun rise on the evil and on the good, and sends rain on the just and on the unjust.'

Matthew v, 43–5

'Pray for those who persecute you'

He does not say: pray that you may not be persecuted. He presumes the persecution is already here and now, already raging, implacable and inescapable, and he says: Pray for those who persecute you. This is the commandment, and it could not be more perfect. In fact, the Lord adds that, if we do this, we are the children of our Father in Heaven, true and worthy children. The Lord himself gave us the example, on the Cross, at the worst moment of the persecution he was suffering, at the very moment of his acceptance of death. His first martyr, and therefore his first witness, St Stephen, behaved in just the same way. From the suffering and for-giveness of Jesus was born our redemption. It may be that from the stoning and prayer of Stephen St Paul was born.

We set too much store by earthly means, and too little by those means which are truly divine. We find it hard to be-lieve that goodness is more powerful, because of its spiritual

16

sway over us and our fellow men, than any direct action or open intervention for ourselves or for others. We do not realize that in order to disarm our enemies—always supposing God wants them to be disarmed—suffering patiently borne, especially if it is suffering inflicted by them, is much more effective than any other weapon of defence or offence.

This does not mean that we must make no effort to avoid injury and persecution. It would be mistaken not to do all in our power to escape the ordeal, and a sign of fatalism and cowardice to abandon ourselves unresistingly to the danger implicit in every trial. But when the hour of persecution has struck, and we can do nothing more with the worldly means at our disposal, then it is that we can do all 'For when I am weak, then I am strong.'[1]

Jesus hung on the Cross, from which only death could release him, and in that moment conquered death and vanquished sin. Stephen fell lifeless under the hail of stones; his eyes, closing for ever to the sunlight, saw the eternal light of Heaven: Paul, standing by, was born a Christian, was born a saint, and what a saint!

In these days when so many members of the Church are being persecuted we must ask ourselves if we have ever prayed for their persecutors. Oh we talk about it, we are always talking about it, but have we ever prayed for them? And if we have not, what sort of Christians are we? How can we honour our Father who makes the same sun shine upon them as upon us, and causes the same rain to fall on their fields as on ours? We Christians are in constant danger of letting ourselves be stunned by the clamour of the world in which we live, and of which, alas, we too form part. We let ourselves be poisoned by the same hatred, the same repugnance, the same cowardly or vindictive passions. We complain, not so much about the spiritual harm done to us by our enemies, as about the bodily discomfort they cause us. We do not think—we refuse to think, so scatter-brained we are! —that, even without persecution and persecutors, our life is naturally woven of pain as well as joy, and death looks over our shoulders.

1. II Corinth. xii, 10.

A.G.&G.—B

Perhaps we hate our persecutors, not so much because they hurt us, and do evil, as because they shake us out of a false conception of life, false but convenient, false, but one which enables us to acquiesce in sin.

If persecutions and persecutors were no longer with us, would there not still be illnesses, disillusions, and death?

Let us pray for those who persecute us, not because they do well to maltreat us, but because, unless we are too stupid to understand, they do us, willy-nilly, a greater service than those who flatter and corrupt us.

4

'*And when evening came, the boat was out on the sea, and he was alone on the land. And he saw that they were distressed in rowing, for the wind was against them. And about the fourth watch of the night he came to them, walking on the sea. He meant to pass by them, but when they saw him walking on the sea they thought it was a ghost and cried out, for they all saw him, and were terrified. But immediately he spoke to them and said: "Take heart, it is I, have no fear." And he got into the boat with them and the wind ceased.*'

Mark vi, 47–51

'They thought it was a ghost'

We too, Lord Jesus, we too so often think of you as a ghost. We are not so eager to know all about you as we are to know other things, everything else. We are not curious to know more about you, any more than we are curious to know more about our souls, ghosts too, as far as we are concerned.

When we are ill, gravely ill, the ghost of our soul rises before our staring terrified eyes, and we cannot banish it. In fact, the ghost of our soul becomes the true, the only, the one reality, while the world, the earth, worldly fame and earthly wealth fade into ghosts. Only then is the soul no longer a ghost, nor is the Lord a ghost. We see him as a present and imminent reality. Then all around us the fading lights of earth no longer shine and sparkle, reflected in our hearts.

19

Jesus alone is real, he has become the only reality. Then there is no other light—there is nothing else.

This transformation takes place, not only during grave illness but also in hours of severe trial. Then we cannot give heed to anyone or anything else. In those cruel moments we no longer turn to men as to our dear and welcome accomplices; they either come as our accusers, or they stay away. Pleasure no longer acts as an all-powerful and infallible lever; there is no more enjoyment to be got out of doing evil; none of the cowardly and common excuses which we so easily accepted avails us now; the whole mechanism we had set up for our safety has crumbled to pieces. All the created world seems hostile to us—it is like a pit from which, once fallen in, we can no longer escape, and when we cry out from its depth there is no one to answer our cry because when there is dire need no one passes by. When the hour of reckoning comes the prisoner, the bankrupt, the criminal caught in the act, the trickster discovered, strike terror into every heart. When this moment comes, a man has no one left beside him but God: he either swears at him as the sole author of his misfortunes, or he prays to him as the only saviour who is never ashamed of anyone or anything, who knows only how to forgive, forgive all, forgive utterly.

For the rest of our lives Jesus is for us a ghost. When we pray to him our prayer is the most listless, slovenly thing we ever offer. We remember him out of a sense of obligation. Every time we have to do something for him, for him alone, it is an infinite bore. And yet no one is more real, more near, more powerful and more friendly than God!

We cling to what eludes us, and stains and ruins us; we neglect you, O Lord, you who alone remain with us, who alone cleanse us from our besetting sins and save us from ourselves.

5

'*Then Jesus was led up by the Spirit into the wilderness to be
tempted by the devil. And he fasted forty days and forty
nights, and afterwards he was hungry. And the tempter came
and said to him, "If you are the Son of God, command these
stones to become loaves of bread," but he answered, "It is
written:*

> '*Man shall not live by bread alone, but by
> every word that proceeds from the mouth of God.*' "

*Then the devil took him to the holy city, and set him on the
pinnacle of the temple, and said to him, "If you are the Son
of God, throw yourself down; for it is written:*

> '*He will give his angels charge of you,*' and
> '*On their hands they will bear you up, lest
> you strike your foot against a stone.*' "

*Jesus said to him, "Again it is written: 'You shall not tempt
the Lord your God.' " *'

Matthew iv, 1–7

'. . . the devil . . . set him on the pinnacle of the temple'

It was an act of daring sacrilege for the devil to lay hands
on Jesus himself, and, as if that were not enough, to raise

21

him to the highest pinnacle of the temple, which means the
house of God, and there murmur in his ear that he should
cast himself down to the ground from that great height. And
all this with the specious excuse of faith in God, love for
God. The devil proves himself a devil by his very insolence,
the brash boldness with which he enters and meddles with
the most sacred things, the most chaste thoughts and the
most sacrosanct persons. He feels a certain wistful attrac-
tion to holiness; it must draw him like a lost treasure, for
when we have lost something we loved, and despair of ever
finding it again, we hate it and plot against it, and attack it
in everyone who still possesses it and every place where it
yet survives.

If he felt no awe of the Lord, of the temple and of the love
for God, he certainly will feel no awe of us. He will, as need
arises, present himself as our professor of theology or spiritual director. When we turn to sin of our own desire he will
leave us alone; there is no need to come to our aid—we
shall bring about our own downfall. But if, by an unusual
chance, we are absorbed in prayer and in the effort to lead
an austere life, then he rubs his hands with glee and comes
up to us and begins to talk. He leads us into church, into the
very sanctuary itself, and proposes deeds of heroism of the
sort that he proposed to Jesus.

Certainly he will not tell us, as he told Jesus, to fling ourselves headlong into the void. He had some suspicion of who
Jesus was, but did not know for sure. He did not know
that Jesus had already made a far greater descent, the descent of which St Paul speaks, from being God's Son to taking on the form of a servant and slave, a fall from God to
man, indeed to the humblest of men. If the devil had known
all about this he would not have dared. He had his doubts—
but in any case he realized that with Jesus he was gambling
dangerously. The stakes were enormous, risky but dazzling.
With us he does not have to make such grand proposals. He
can indulge in frivolous suggestions that must make him
smile: a pay rise, promotion in our career, a puff to our
vanity, a momentary meanness, an angry harshness to our

inferiors, a deceitful plot against a superior, a patent injustice which can yet be covered up, without exposing us to dishonour; detraction of others, that we contrive with a thousand pretexts but without a single valid reason; a dishonest thought which we do not banish at once but play with, blindfold, until we fall into ignominy, betrayed by a single glance or word—these, and others like these, are the snares he sets for us.

Although it is merely a retail trade that the devil carries on with us, he always arrives when we are on the pinnacle of the temple, fresh from confession and penance, observing a period of abstinence, or doing some good work. We never see ourselves in such a wicked light as when we are being virtuous. If we pray, all our most reprehensible thoughts flock into our minds at that hour. If we do a kind deed to our neighbour, he seems unbearable to us. If we deny ourselves a lawful pleasure, we feel like fanatics or, even worse, fools. On the contrary, when we do something wrong, then our heart takes wings and seems full of the noblest thoughts and most angelic intentions. Oh, how devilish the devil is—how cunningly he chooses the highest peaks! The more we draw away from him the more he pursues us. But the word of God—if we did but live according to it—always shuts his mouth. The devil may still come near, but he can never get the better of us, if the word of God rises to our lips, and if it springs from our hearts.

6

*'Then the King will say to those at his right hand, "Come,
O blessed of my Father, inherit the kingdom prepared for
you from the foundation of the world; for I was hungry and
you gave me food, I was thirsty and you gave me drink, I
was a stranger and you welcomed me, I was naked and you
clothed me, I was sick and you visited me, I was in prison
and you came to me!" Then the righteous will answer him,
"Lord, when did we see thee hungry and feed thee, thirsty
and give thee drink? And when did we see thee a stranger
and welcome thee, or naked and clothe thee? And when did
we see thee sick or in prison and visit thee?" And the King
will answer them, "Truly, I say to you, as you did it to one
of the least of these my brethren, you did it to me." '*

Matthew xxv, 34–40

'You did it to me'

When a poor man comes up to me and begs for bread, and
I repel him with an excuse and a look of annoyance, I repel
Jesus. When I prefer a rich, powerful, intelligent and well-
dressed man to a human creature debased by ignorance, sin,
hardship and disease, I prefer the rich man to Jesus. When,
in conversation with others, I criticize my neighbour harshly
for his mistakes or wrongdoing, I am dealing harshly with
Jesus. When, for the sake of a luxurious, or merely an easy,
life, I sacrifice my conscience, and perhaps even my voca-
tion for an austere and devout life, I sacrifice Jesus.

24

We have the impudence to persuade ourselves that we cannot see Jesus. Who knows? He may not even exist! We have never met him. We would like to meet him. What a welcome we would give him! He would be our loved and honoured guest, and would stay with us for ever. What cowards we are! Of course Jesus is here; we see him even too often. 'He stood in the midst of them!'[1] He was there, he is here today, and will always be here. Jesus is present in all who suffer, all who hunger and thirst, even in the sinner who goes to prison; he said so himself. He is here in the tortured flesh, the grieving soul, the broken heart, in the child born weeping, the old man who dies alone, and the woman who is insulted and afflicted.

We call ourselves Christians, but we are many other things first; only at the last moment, and if there is still time, are we Christians. Before then we belong to this or that family, this or that city, this or that ideology. We are working men or professional people, farmers or clerks, poor folk or rich. First of all we have our own likes and dislikes, and where do we put them? Right in the forefront. Even the poorest and humblest of men has his own likes and dislikes, and is prepared to sacrifice everything and everyone else in order to satisfy even one of these. So, when do we begin to be Christians, real Christians? Perhaps at the moment of our death. Then when we can no longer be anything else—then we are Christians—there is nothing else for us to be. At long last we see Jesus. And Jesus might well say to us: 'So, it's you, is it? At this late hour?'

Jesus is within us too, within our body and soul. He is in every one of us, as in every one of our fellow men. And we who never see him, even within ourselves, insult our soul with frivolous thoughts, vain pursuits, foolish whims and unworthy affections. When we do this we insult Jesus. We subject our body, with the excuse of satisfying it, to excesses and corruption, disease and infirmities, and so dishonour it. In so doing we dishonour Jesus. We treat ourselves with incredible scorn and cruelty. We grudge our soul a little pure

1. John i, 26.

water to drink, a moment's peace, the joy of being recollected with God and with other souls. We are always there by its side, pricking it, soiling it, compromising and exasperating it, content with the meagre rest we find in sleep, the only respite we grant our soul too. We make use of the soul in our business dealings, in our philosophizing over a passion, in the way we ill-treat our friends and overcome our enemies and outstrip them. The soul has to do all we ask of it. We have reduced it to a state of slavery, with no rights and no time off.

As for our body, we treat that no more wisely. In a certain sense we kill it ourselves, with our own hands. It must eat and drink whatever we happen to like at any given moment, not what is good for us—which would be so frugal and so simple. It must be kept slaving away without light or rest, yet very little labour would satisfy all our needs. Alas! where we do not succeed in doing evil ourselves others succeed only too well; socially, all of us together, we have made Hell out of our life here. There are even men who make their fortunes out of cornering other men's labour, their wealth from others' need.

It is almost as if we were all mad, diabolical, unbelievable —yet these are realities of our daily life. We need so little to live, very little indeed; yet we never manage to get it, and so many die of hunger.

Why do we not see that Jesus still suffers in every one of us? We go on cheerfully imprisoning him, scourging him, crowning him with thorns, spitting in his face, striking and mocking him, wounding him and laying the most intolerable burden upon him, and at last hounding him to death. What do we do but slay Jesus in ourselves and in our fellows?

7

*'And Jesus entered the temple of God and drove out all who
sold and bought in the temple, and he overturned the tables
of the money changers and the seats of those who sold pigeons.
He said to them, "It is written: My house shall be called a
house of prayers, but you make it a den of robbers." . . . And
leaving them he went out of the city to Bethany and lodged
there.'*

Matthew xxi, 10–17

'He went out of the city to Bethany, and lodged there'

We do not intend, like so many of our contemporary
writers, to inveigh against the towns as such: the octopus
towns with their grasping tentacles, the monstrous towns,
the human whirlpools, the cities that devour men and women.
The truth is that at the present time the town has spread
everywhere. Even the most famous resorts at the seaside, in
the valleys, on the mountain peaks or in the hills, have taken
on the aspect of towns. If they did not look like towns, if they
did not have some of the features of towns, no one would visit
them. We flee from the town . . . to go to the town: a town
set in the countryside, but still a town. Everything has become
town—we cannot escape it.

From this story told by St Matthew it would appear that
our Lord liked to 'lodge' in the country. He 'entered Jerusalem' but he 'lodged' in the country. Perhaps we may see in

27

this preference of his a lesson, or at least a suggestion, for us all. The country is good, not only for our bodily health but also for our souls. To hear us talk one would think we were all body and nothing else, and that our doctors were our new spiritual directors. The air does this or that, the height has this or that effect, the sunlight acts upon us in this way or that, and so on; it is as if we were walking lumps of flesh and nothing else. When people talk of going away for a holiday I never hear them say that one place is more advisable than another for their soul's sake.

Yet the country, as distinct from the town, has much to give to our souls as well as to our bodies. The town is entirely man's work, the triumph of his labour. The country remains, and will always remain, the work of God. It is a great boon for the Christian soul to leave the mean and pretentious works of men and seek the works of God, so modest and so grand. We enter a new spiritual land when we go into the country.

First of all, it is a land of silence. The myriad voices of the wind and water, of all the living creatures, do not break this silence, they animate it. It is a living silence. The town is never silent: when, in the early morning hours, its noises die away, their absence makes us afraid; it is the silence of a graveyard. The houses, all full of living people asleep, are like so many tombs. If we go through the town during those hours our hearts are not inspired with fine thoughts—they are filled with disquiet. Instead, the silence of the countryside is like a song that never ends, and is always new.

The country is full of light. In the towns we have achieved the unimaginable horror of living in rows of neatly cemented square stone boxes; even at noon we live by electric light. But in the country there is light even after sunset. I know of nothing so illuminating as a night spent watching in the open countryside.

It is true that in the country we are at the mercy of the elements. In the towns we have so cushioned ourselves with comforts that to compare a countryman with a townsman is like comparing a healthy man with an invalid. The rough conditions of the open country are what we need to keep fit in body and soul—yes, what we need for our soul. In the country a man is aware of the mystery of life and feels that life eludes his grasp; instead, in the town he feels all-powerful and 'on top of the world'. Yet he has no power at all, except to hasten his own destruction.

Perhaps there was good reason for Holy Scripture to say that the cities were invented by Cain.[1]

1. cf. Genesis iv, 17.

8

'Then some of the scribes and Pharisees said to him: "Teacher, we wish to see a sign from you." But he answered them: "An evil and adulterous generation seeks for a sign; but no sign shall be given to it. . . ." '

Matthew xiii, 38–9

'We wish to see a sign from you'

There is nothing ironical or ridiculous in the definition of man as 'an animal that wants to see everything'. It is quite true. His eternal happiness will consist wholly in the vision of God, who is infinite: there is no fear that at a certain moment a man may have seen everything and have nothing more to discover. Instead, here below novelty is fickle, it does not last; our eyes grow dull and weary as we gaze at customary everyday things. So it is not surprising that Jesus was asked to give a 'sign', that is, perform a miracle. It would have been something new. We pass our time hoping for something new. This means we are not content with anything we already have.

It is also true that a man usually feels and knows that his fellows, more often than not, cheat him, as he himself, more often than not, cheats others; we are always setting little snares for each other.

A miracle is something different—at least something other than ourselves is at work, something that has nothing in com-

30

mon with our own wretched reasoning or cunning, which is
outside the customary ugly round. A miracle is not only a
new thing, it is a thing of beauty like a new radiance out-
shining a thousand stars; the miracle is a flash of light. It is
only a gleam, but it is from God, and from the divine world.
No wonder we run to see it! We run to see a new spectacle
of our unending passions, a new story of our perpetual
vicissitudes, a new face or a new voice. Anything outside the
common run of our days, hours and ways brings us to a sud-
den halt. At once we gather in a little knot around two braw-
lers, a broken-down car, a fallen horse, a strange poster, a
more than usually preposterous quack, a striking display in a
shop window, a Punch and Judy show, a funeral procession
or a jaunty tune. The children who run after street musicians,
the women who gather in their doorways or at their windows,
the men who pause, still thoughtful but with more cheerful
thoughts, as if they felt some relief, are only doing what we
all do. Why do we like a new poet, a new painter, a new car
or a new dress? Whether young or old, every man, and every
woman too, no doubt, is stirred by something new. It shakes
us out of our dreary round, the daily chores of our common
life. Its great power of distraction lies in the way it sets us
free from all that we are accustomed to—and every departure
is a joy.

They wanted to see Jesus perform a miracle, and it was not
this which made him angry. He was angry because they de-
manded a certain kind of miracle, not the kind we all ought
to ask him for. We all want miracles, it is true, but not those
which help us along the steep and narrow road to Heaven:
rather those which cheer us on the wide open way to Hell.
We would all like God to help us to live far away from him.
This is the error, in fact the horror, of our desires. We are
quite capable of asking God for the grace of humiliating our
persecutor, striking down our enemy, increasing our wealth,
and maintaining our good health, lest it should be worn down
and ruined by vice. There was once a drunkard who begged
our Lady to grant that he might grow old without ever having
to give up a single glass; he wanted to die in good form, to

remain a wine hero till the end. Now he was a poor fool, foolish by nature, and made more foolish by alcohol; but if we start thinking about our own prayers we see ourselves mirrored in them. We only ask God for those things which keep us well away from him.

We want to have him at our command, not to place ourselves at his. Foolish wretches that we are, we want him to become like us; we do not want to become like him. He became Man, but that does not satisfy us: we would like him to become like such or such a man, unmindful of God and ignorant of himself, like me, or you, like us all. We would like to see miracles, not of salvation but of perdition, not miracles of well doing but miracles of well being. A dreadful crime—this sounds impossible but it is true—impresses us, and secretly we admire the thief who has got away, or the ambitious man who has succeeded. Victorious vice fills us with admiration and awe. When Jesus multiplies the loaves we would like to make him our king, but when he hangs on the Cross we leave him and join the ranks of those who crucify him.

This is our mistake, this is our guilt. We want to see miracles, but we do not like those which open to us the gates of Heaven. We like miracles, but we do not like God.

9

'*And Jesus went away from there and withdrew to the district of Tyre and Sidon. And behold, a Canaanite woman from that region came out and cried, "Have mercy on me, O Lord, Son of David, my daughter is severely possessed by a demon." But he did not answer her a word. And his disciples came and begged him, saying, "Send her away, for she is crying after us." He answered, "I was sent only to the lost sheep of the house of Israel." But she came and knelt before him, saying, "Lord, help me." And he answered, "It is not fair to take the children's bread and throw it to the dogs." She said, "Yes, Lord, yet even the dogs eat the crumbs that fall from their Master's table." Then Jesus answered her, "O woman, great is your faith. Be it done for you as you desire." And her daughter was healed instantly.*'

Matthew xv, 21–8

'Be it done for you as you desire'

If only the Lord would say these words, or something like them, to one of us! If he would grant this almighty power to us also, even if it were to be but for a single wish, or a single moment! If the Lord would only grant our desires, in the way we desire! We should be, if only for a moment, equal to God. Equal in power, certainly, but equal in goodness? But we do not covet his goodness.

And yet, if we think about it, God has given and still gives us much more than this. It is certainly a great grace to be suddenly healed of an inveterate disease that has resisted all attempts to cure it; it is a great grace to see the iron chains of material nature broken for us, a marvellous thing to be the subject of a miracle, and in our own poor flesh receive the marks of direct divine intervention, independent of any secondary cause. But God has performed for us, and still performs, miracles incomparably greater than these. He is always waiting to bestow upon us powers far greater and more impressive than the power of healing.

To begin with an example: Lazarus was raised from the dead. A great miracle, undoubtedly. A few years later he died again, this time without any hope of rising before the last day of the final and universal resurrection. What mattered most to him? to be raised from the dead, by means of an almost incredible miracle, to live for a few years longer, or to have met Jesus, known him, believed in him and loved him? What mattered more to him, to live a little longer on earth, or to be saved in eternity? And which is the greater miracle, to restore the blind to sight, or to forgive sins?

Have we ever thought of what this means—the forgiveness of sin, the conversion of the sinner? We are so accustomed to the material life that we do not realize what the life of the spirit is, indeed we do not even know that it exists, or why. The resurrection from sin is a much greater grace than the resurrection from death, and the restoration of friendship with God is much more miraculous than the restoration of a dead man to life. Sin, in its own nature, and apart from the mercy of God, deserves to be punished by God's justice instantly, without remission and for eternity. Sin is death, real death, eternal death. And yet we rise again from sin, and this resurrection is in our own hands. 'Be it done for you as you desire.'

But that is not all. To be able to love God, or even to pray to him as a Father, praying with the heart of a son, a real and loving son albeit by adoption only, is a miracle that, as St Paul says, can only be worked in us by the Spirit of God. Below the surface of our earthly and mortal life there is in us a divine life which is full of miracles, in every moment of which Jesus says to us 'Be it done for you as you desire.'

The strange thing is that we do not wish to live this life, we cling fiercely to our external and temporal existence which, bound and controlled by the laws of matter, made up of blind actions and reactions, seems to us, who are made up of spirit and matter, sinister and cruel. Nevertheless, this is the only life that satisfies us, keeps us closely attached to it—the only life we care about.

Our Lord, instead, tries in every way and by every means to lead us into the true life. His conversation, one might almost say his altercation, with the Canaanite woman, reported by St Matthew (chap. xv, 21–8) reveals the Lord's intentions and methods. With a few stern retorts he leads her on to an avowal of that great faith which he could answer in no other way than with the words he used: 'Be it done for you as you desire.' He is about to restore her daughter's physical health, but meanwhile he reveals to the mother the wonders of the life of God, and teaches her how to share in these. Whereas at first he seems merely to contradict and rebuke her, almost to insult her, in reality he is spurring her on, exciting her, detaching her from a purely material conception of life and enabling her to rise heaven-wards and God-wards until finally he draws from her that cry of perfect humility and fearless love which God can never resist. When he hears it he descends to embrace his creature and gives her everything she desires, even his far-famed almighty power. But a soul in love has no use for power—she is not seeking this when she seeks God.

We have God with us, God for us, and we know neither ourselves nor God; we know nothing about meeting him, or collaborating with him. No miracle is greater than being able to love him; yet this is the miracle that leaves us cold. We shun it as a dangerous thing.

IO

'Now there is in Jerusalem, by the Sheep Gate, a pool, in Hebrew called Beth-zatha, which has five porticos. In these lay a multitude of invalids, blind, lame, paralysed. One man was there, who had been ill for thirty-eight years. When Jesus saw him and knew that he had been lying there a long time, he said to him, "Do you want to be healed?" The sick man answered him, "Sir, I have no man to put me into the pool when the water is troubled, and while I am going another steps down before me." Jesus said to him, "Rise, take up your pallet, and walk." And at once the man was healed, and he took up his pallet and walked. . . . The Jews . . . asked him, "Who is the man who said to you, 'Take up your pallet, and walk?'" Now the man who had been healed did not know who it was, for Jesus had withdrawn, as there was a crowd in the place. Afterwards Jesus found him in the temple. . . .'

John v, 2–14

'the man . . . did not know who it was'

However unlikely and incredible it may seem, the paralysed cripple whom Jesus had healed was so overjoyed by his cure that it never even occurred to him to find out who had healed him, in order to take his hand and ask his name. He cannot have been a wicked man: a short while afterwards Jesus found him again, in the temple. It is true that the temple was the chief meeting-place of the city, the market-place, as Jesus was to say later,[1] but the fact remains that the poor cripple, as soon as he recovered the use of his legs and rejoiced in walking again, rejoiced also in going to the temple to thank God. It was there that he found Jesus, and recognized his healer.

Jesus has given so much to men, and so many of them have never even heard his name. If God, through his Word, created the whole world, do we not owe everything to Jesus? We owe him the universe, as much of it as we can see around us, as much as is contained in ourselves. We owe him our eyes, so often filled with sadness, and our hands which are at times so strong and at other times so faltering, our patient docile feet, and our mysterious and secret flesh; we owe him our hearts which beat in their dark cavity, never stopping by day or night, and the delicate mechanisms of our lungs, and all our senses with their intricate and manifold life. We owe him the lands we live in, the changing light around us, the air we breathe. We owe him our parents, relations and friends. We owe him our enemies, who are perhaps, in spite of the trouble they give us and their continual interference, the most useful of our neighbours. We owe him this or that condition, this or that kind of education, civilization, and sense of life. Nor must we object that many men have nothing of all this. That is untrue. The gift of life itself is such that in any condition it outweighs all sorts of hardship and confinement. No one, in whatever state he may find himself, wishes to die; men always wish to live. Even the most wretched among us feel that life is the greatest boon. Those who complain about living do so to pass the time, or to stir our pity; none of those who invoke death is ever glad to die, and those who have taken their own lives must have done so in a state of deliberate orgasm and self-inflicted madness. One might say they have gone mad on purpose to kill themselves. Well—life was given us by Jesus and through his hands, but how many people are aware of this? Most of the men who lived in past times 'did not know who it was', many now living do not know, and many yet to be born will not know.

1. Luke xix, 46.

There are some who know this: *we* do, we know even more. We know that we owe Jesus not only the life of nature but also the life of grace. We owe it to him, who became our brother, that we have found our Father again and been able to embrace him. We owe it to him that we can once more listen to his divine voice speaking to us from Heaven and from eternity; we owe it to him that we are able to recognize that voice, so far away and yet so near, so powerful and yet so gentle. We owe it to him that our hearts have eagerly answered, and that we have cried out to him from the depths of our misery. He became man in order to lead us, through himself, to our new life which is our old, our eternal life, the only life for us. He became man and united God and man so closely in himself in order that all fear should be banished from our hearts, and all love be born. We know all this. But how do we know it? And are we grateful to him for it? Or do we live as if we were unaware of it? And why do we love everyone else but him?

You may say: But we do love him. Our finest buildings are the churches we have erected for him. The most solemn occasions in our lives are bound and, as it were, sealed with a golden seal, by his word. We revere the rites of his Church. His ministers are our shepherds; his words are our law. All this is true, but is it enough? These expressions of love may or may not be sincere, God alone knows this, but even if they are sincere they are not enough. Jesus wants to be loved, and love is much less and much more than all this. Do we ever think about him? If not, what kind of love is ours? Do we ever try to live a few moments of every hour with him? If not, why do we call it love? Love, real love, gives itself no rest; our so-called love for Jesus leaves us at liberty, even to insult him. . . .

II

'And after six days Jesus took with him Peter and James and John his brother, and led them up a high mountain apart. And he was transfigured before them, and his face shone like the sun, and his garments became white as light. And behold, there appeared to them Moses and Elijah, talking with him. And Peter said to Jesus, "Lord, it is well that we are here; if you wish, I will make three booths here, one for you and one for Moses and one for Elijah." He was still speaking, when lo, a bright cloud overshadowed them, and a voice from the cloud said, "This is my beloved Son, with whom I am well pleased; listen to him." '

Matthew xvii, 1–5

'Listen to him'

This is the Father's command, to all men at all times, yesterday, today and tomorrow. He, the Father, now speaks no more, except through Jesus who is his Word, in time and in eternity. Whoever wishes to hear the Father must hear the Son. But how can we hear him, and why is it so hard?

It is very hard, and also very easy. Very hard: it may even happen that a preacher of his gospel may not be able to hear Jesus, whereas a poor ignorant fool may succeed—and how well he hears him, with such clarity of understanding, such inward acceptance and joy! It is very hard, and it is very easy, and the difficulty and ease spring from the same source:

39

the presence or absence of good will. When Jesus was born the angels sang that his birth meant glory to God and peace to men 'of good will', not to all men, only to those 'of good will'. We know what will is, and what good will is, too; and yet it is a fact that although we know this it is as if we did not know it because we do not know it in practice.

The will is not desire, or inclination; it is not a longing or a whim, it is not even one of those forces which compel us almost inevitably to act, as if by compulsion—so strong and pressing they are, and (it seems to us) so irresistible. These forces arise from instinct and passion combined with vice, which is an inveterate habit. The will is something else. It is the spiritual force which is born of reason and which can and must contain, control and direct all these other forces which drive us to action. It is of its nature the strongest force; it is unfortunately also the weakest, because of our foolishness and negligence, our guilty blindness and servitude, our lack of virtue.

Virtue is, in fact, nothing else but the will directed towards its true end, towards what constitutes its necessary fulfilment. Virtue is born when the will obeys, not the blind impulses of the instinct and the senses, but right reason. A virtuous man exercises his will power effectively, and so does what his intelligence demands. Naturally, it is not only the will that must be free from error, above all from wilful, and therefore blameworthy, error. When the will is enslaved to the lower forces it constrains the understanding too, either not to see, or to see falsely. In this terrible interior conflict it is wonderful enough if the man can vanquish and tame the animal; imagine what it must be for the Christian to control and save the man!

What happens most frequently is that the passions tyrannize over the reason, especially in the roughest and least civilized men, and we know how rough and uncivilized are many of those who, because of their great wealth, acquire an air of culture and refinement. And with men who have exercised their brains in a special field of knowledge the reason becomes proud and aggressive, like a passion—or even more

—so that to oblige it to yield to faith and grace requires a miracle, and a divine miracle. It is much easier to convert a man of corrupt senses than a man of corrupt mind, because mental vices are in this world accepted as so many virtues, and acclaimed as such.

So to have a good will is no mean matter, and demands no mean effort. Nobody is entirely good, or good always and for ever; when we speak of a good man we are thinking of such goodness as can be found on earth among men. Without a good will there is no peace, that peace which we need in order to listen to the voice of Jesus. And he alone can speak to us the essential words, the words of salvation. To hear him and to obey means to be saved. 'Listen to him.'

What are we doing, in order to obtain a good will to set at the helm of our life? Nothing. And yet this is the only thing we can have for the asking, the only way by which we can make friends with God, that is, be saved. We do our best to succeed in this or that enterprise, and we think we have become Heaven knows what when we have become, shall we say, successful business men, bankers, general managers, great writers, famous preachers or actors, great clowns, popular athletes, and so on. Sometimes we are more modest: to make a little money, take a step forward in our career, cut a fine figure with a superior, or see our colleagues bursting with envy—this is bliss. And to obtain this we are prepared to sacrifice health, dignity and conscience. We wear ourselves out, sometimes even to death. Thus engaged in such tragic futilities, how can we be bothered to attend to our interior life? In fact, the man who cares about the life of his soul, seriously cares, putting it before everything else, is called by one name only: a 'saint'.

Only the saints listen to Jesus. To listen to him even once means never leaving him again. His is not a voice that can be forgotten: when we hear it, even for a moment, we cannot live without it.

12

'Lo, a bright cloud overshadowed them, and a voice from the cloud said, "This is my beloved Son, with whom I am well pleased...."'

Matthew xvii, 5

'A bright cloud . . .'

This may be merely a poetical or picturesque image, but strangely enough, by an irresistible association of ideas, it makes us think of faith. Faith may be described as a cloud; a cloud lit by the sun which it alternately hides and reveals, the sun to which it is daughter and shield, the sun which does not scatter it but pierces and pervades it. In fact, what is faith if not knowledge which cannot express all its evidence and light in its own terms, because it is authoritatively revealed to us by God, and so receives all its radiance from him and reflects this divine light upon us?

We very often find in the sacred books, and consequently in Christian writers and artists, the image and symbol of a cloud. I dare say that the fact that the cloud has been popular with some of the greatest poets, unbelievers included, of past times may be due to their familiarity with the Bible, which these writers had at their fingertips and studied as the primary source of poetry and truth. We do not need to insert here a string of quotations from sacred or profane literature, for we are not indulging in a literary exercise; we wish merely to

use this analogy as the starting point of less poetical but more
real considerations. We can see the Lord, and all that pertains
to him, only through a cloud, a cloud which rises from our
earthly condition, the cloud of our essential participation in
the world of matter, the cloud of our being, largely animal
and physical. All our knowledge is linked to our senses, and
smacks of these; even our intellectual knowledge cannot go
beyond certain limits, those of our own nature. Our knowledge
of God cannot be anything but fragmentary, being attained
by a process of excluding this and that—shutting out all that
is finite and measured or measurable. We must consider also
that our intelligence, with our whole nature, has been raised
to the supernatural state, and is therefore, in a certain sense,
much more than a merely natural intelligence. On the other
hand, our intelligence, and our whole nature with it, has
been stained and wounded by original sin, and is therefore
far inferior to a bright and healthy human intelligence. So we
shall understand why many of these truths of faith, especially
those which we call mysteries, are not, and cannot be, to our
eyes anything but clouds suffused with light. And it is a good
thing that they seem to us like clouds because our vision, in
its present state, could not bear the sight of those truths
naked and exposed; their radiance would dazzle us.

. . . . .

A cloudless sky seems to stretch further away, but it is less
beautiful. One might almost say it has little to say to us.
Clouds are constantly changing their shapes and colours,
every one is different from its fellows, not one remains the
same for long; they are rather like our thoughts, our affections and our souls. Clouds are always clouds, and we are
always men—and yet what variety, what play of light and
shade, what new portents, what depth or grace of changing
forms, what beauty and what power of assembly and of
merry chase through the air! A sky that is always serene,
unruffled by even a puff of wind, has a melancholy effect in
the end; it suggests a glass eye, an inhuman fixity of gaze,

changeless, spell-bound, crystalline. With the variety of their dark, fierce onslaughts and delicate fleecy forms, the brightest, rarest colours and the palest, most transparent tints, the solitude of a single cloud high in the Heavens, and the moving ranks of massed vapours, the clouds are like the music of Heaven. They resemble our affections and our thoughts which, like them, leave no trace. Where are the thoughts I had yesterday? and the memories, fancies and dreams, ideas and tender affections of a day that is gone? Every day in my soul has had its clouds and I have lived so many days, and all have come and gone! But where did they go, those clouds which were the life and colour of my days, of so many days? and how many of them were bathed in the light of God?

O Lord, have pity on us, and on all the events of our lives, so often futile and obscure!

Let your light fall on the clouds which rise and run their race beneath our low and darkened skies. The light we see is only what is reflected or mirrored; we see only in riddles. You, the sun of our being, can reach us only through our screen of clouds. Shine through their thick entangled veils, O Jesus. We know that your light cannot be revealed in time, but only in eternity; we know that our eyes, small, weak, made of flesh and foredoomed to death, cannot bear your direct rays. O Lord, we beg you to pierce through the rifts of our mortality, the barriers of our infirmities, the earthly veils, the worldly vapours. Have pity on us, do not leave us a single day without some of your light, even if only reflected upon us. And even in the most anguished moments, most clouded and most exhausted, make our terrified hearts feel that you are still here, though unseen, and that you will shine again in splendour. Above all, that you will return at the end of our days, in a different splendour, when our mortality is swallowed up in death. Come, Lord Jesus.

13

'Again he said to them, "I go away, and you will seek me and die in your sin; where I am going, you cannot come." Then said the Jews, "Will he kill himself, since he says, 'Where I am going, you cannot come'?" He said to them, "You are from below, I am from above; you are of this world, I am not of this world. I told you that you would die in your sins unless you believe that I am he." They said to him, "Who are you?" Jesus said to them, "Even what I have told you from the beginning." '

John viii, 21–5

'You will die in your sin'

Today it is the fashion to be flippant about religion. In the past we were humanists, now we are humanitarians. Today, in this age of universal and social redemption, a Christian finds it most embarrassing to mention Hell. In order to remain at our ease, and to weaken or even abolish the sense of sin, we have set up philosophies and psychologies to our own liking. According to these, sin is a negative attitude of the mind, and when a positive attitude is acquired we obtain the necessary synthesis: this is the life of the spirit, the dialectic of life. So say the philosophers, the idealists. Instead the psychologists, the acknowledged heirs of all that remains of positivism, assert that in the sense of sin we must discern one of the most fatal flaws in our psychic development; from this

45

and from nowhere and nothing else is derived every sort of spiritual malady; therefore it must be eradicated, especially in children, cautiously but resolutely. The sense of sin—how disgusting! Life is joy, let it not be dimmed: so say the doctors of our mentally sick.

These worthy folk ennoble with their theories—we must hope with innocent intentions if not with outstanding intelligence—what is neither more nor less than irresponsibility and ignorance. God may forgive them, but when he forgives he does not arrest or wipe out the effects of the evil they have set in motion. God forgives, but history does not forgive, the dialectic of the spirit and the development of the psyche (to borrow the theoretical formulæ of their religions) do not forgive. God may pardon a repentant murderer, but the murdered man is not restored to life, he is dead and gone, and the terrible consequences of a murder will be felt in men's minds and in their material interests. Who can say what evil is accumulated by those vain theories which, with the excuse of setting our minds at rest, lull us into danger and promise us impunity in temptation?

The Lord will surely come in his own time, and how shall we answer him? Shall we say we subscribed to this or that Review, were followers of this or that leader, and thought in such or such a manner? These are answers we can give to each other, and we do not even believe them ourselves; we pretend to believe them, in order that others may believe our own. They are not the sort of answers we can give to God. The human conscience is not a wilderness of sophistry or a midden of ancestral and bestial filth, as these worthy folk want us to believe; our conscience is the vision granted to us as creatures of God, creatures who are largely spiritual and outside the laws of matter, creatures capable of loving God and being loved by him, creatures of time and of eternity. We can drug our consciences but we cannot destroy them.

So death will surely come, and how can we hope to do then what we find so hard to do now, that is, be converted? How can we, when our bodies are stupefied with pain and racked with fever, or robbed of all strength—how can we then at long

last be converted? It is nonsensical. If there is a time when
our soul is distracted it is just then, when physical pain ab-
sorbs its attention. On the point of dying, even if we are in
time to understand that we are near to death, we shall be
thinking only of what we can do to avoid it. They will not
tell us that there is no more hope, and even if they were to
say this we would not be convinced. Until our last breath we
shall still hope to live. We shall die blindfold. The light of
eternity will be shed upon us, and all around us, and yet we
shall still be thinking of living in terms of time—a moment,
just a moment longer.

Let us not deceive ourselves. If we live in sin we shall die
in sin. We die as we live, and the last act of our lives will be
like all the preceding acts. 'In your sins you will die.' If we
love sin we live and die in it. Even almighty God can do
nothing about it, because he respects our free will, and our
free will has chosen sin. Money, masses of it, more and more
money, higher and more ambitious honours; glory, fame and
flattery; pleasures, more and more sophisticated, and pursued
to the point of suffering, even to the border of vice (but with
impunity); the incorrigible pride of place on this earth, whence
all passes away—and even if everything else should remain,
we would pass away—this is the material of our death. With
what little bit of soul still clings to us, the final crisis will be
dreadful; if we think of God we shall be tempted to hate him,
curse him and blaspheme. Death will be the beginning of
Hell.

Before this life ends Hell will have begun.

14

'But you are not to be called rabbi, for you have one teacher, and you are all brethren. And call no man your father on earth, for you have one Father, who is in Heaven. Neither be called masters, for you have one master, the Christ. He who is greatest among you shall be your servant; whoever exalts himself will be humbled, and whoever humbles himself will be exalted.'

Matthew xxiii, 8–12

'Your servant'

Let us think for a moment; the whole story of individual men, and of mankind in general, to judge by some recent theories, is like a grand highway, very often a Way of the Cross, or an Appian Way flanked with tombs, or rather with ruins and the remains of tombs. The road of freedom, as they say. According to these theories men have been doing nothing else but advance along this painful and glorious way. And this is true, as long as we are speaking of men's spiritual liberty, but when we consider the liberty of the rest of his being we see that he is imprisoned by physical and physiological laws, in a way that frightens us whenever we think about it. Not only am I ignorant of why I ever came into the world (after all, I wasn't there to know the reason why), but I do not even know when, how, or why I shall leave it. In a matter of such importance for me I ought to have been consulted and informed; someone should have asked my opinion and allowed me to express my wishes. But no: I cannot know the hour or way of my departure. And as for staying on here and living, I may give myself all the airs I wish, and make the most wonderful discoveries, but nevertheless the physical conditions of my existence depend only to a slight extent on me. The famous work that is of such great importance is really but a trifle, compared with my respiration, nourishment and the circulation of my blood—all things of capital importance to me which come about without the slightest effort on my part. If I stop to think about them I may disturb and alter these innocent and instinctive functions; if I think of the pleasures of the table, or of sport, or of every other kind of pleasure, I see what kind of 'work' I give myself.

The body is not only in prison, it is itself a prison, the prison of the soul. Does the soul enjoy more freedom? Certainly. It is not free in its intelligence, which cannot avoid seeing what it sees and cannot alter; but it is free in the will. Free will creates our spiritual freedom, individually and socially. We do not want to discuss here the measure and the conditions of this freedom; we want merely to assert that very often this freedom, considered in itself, seems an empty thing, a form without content, a force without direction. Freedom finds its fulfilment in an affection, that is, in something which pleases us, and to which we consecrate our lives. If, for example, I love God and my neighbour, why is it that at once, as if by instinct, I place myself at the service of God and of my neighbour? I do not try to get rid of them, I try to serve them. St Paul dared to say of Jesus, that is, of the Son of God, that he not only made himself Man, but, as if that were not enough—he became a servant. St Paul makes no bones about it: he 'took the form of a servant'.[1] The same thing happens in any love, of any kind: we become the slaves of those we love.

We must then admit that men seem to follow not one road but two, one that leads towards freedom, and another that leads to servitude. The one leads to freedom from violence,

1. Philippians ii, 7.

A.G.&G.—D

injustice and hatred; the other to freedom from selfishness, pride and self-sufficiency. We do not seek merely to recover our liberty, we wish to consecrate it to something; we should be unworthy of the name of men if we remained in the service and slavery of the powerful, the overbearing and the violent; nor should we be men if our liberty did not lead us to the service of our Father in Heaven and our brothers on earth.

'Minister' means servant; we have made of it a pre-eminent and supreme name, a dignity, an authority, a high ornamental throne approached by many steps. Poor men as we are, we create vanity, gain and pride even out of humility, poverty and the starkness of reality. Jesus was a servant, the saints were servants, we are servants ourselves as soon as our affections are engaged; servants of love, to be sure, but under obedience till death. Let us not be afraid of being servants, or of the mockery of this progressive century; when there is love, real love, we are its servants, and this servitude to love is true freedom. If we want to be sure who and what it is we love, it is very easy to find out; we must see who and what it is we serve. There can be no mistake: it is an infallible test and proof.

15

'Then the mother of the sons of Zebedee came up to him,
with her sons, and kneeling before him she asked him for
something. And he said to her, "What do you want?"
She said to him, "Command that these two sons of mine
may sit, one at your right hand and one at your left, in
your kingdom." But Jesus answered, "You do not know
what you are asking. Are you able to drink the cup that I
am to drink?" They said to him, "We are able." He said
to them, "You will drink my cup, but to sit at my right
hand and at my left is not mine to grant, but it is for those
for whom it has been prepared by my Father." '

Matthew xx, 20–3

'It is not mine to grant'

Jesus is indeed the judge of the living and the dead, but
at his second coming, not his first. When he came first he
was one of us; he did not distribute rewards for valour,
he fought alongside us, in the same trench.

Philosophers of great repute have reproached Christianity
for preaching a utilitarian morality, entirely based on gain,
rewards and prizes. True morality, the philosophers have said,
keeps well away from awards and penalties; it is pure. Pure
morality, pure reason, pure love, pure poetry—recent centuries have been waging wars to keep everything pure, and
never before have we been so filthy, so stained with mire and

our brothers' blood. In any case, those high-minded philosophers have never pondered over this Gospel language, or understood that Heaven is not a toy promised to a child to dissuade him from crying. It is not a gold medal pinned on a hero's chest, or a public monument erected to the glory of a great man; strictly speaking, it is not even a prize. It is the final goal, the concluding stage, of our spiritual development, in a word, our end. We were created for no other purpose: our reward consists in our perfect, full and absolute fulfilment of this end.

Jesus lays stress upon our share in his suffering, not upon the benefits we shall draw from it. It is as if he is telling us not to be lured away from our immediate task in this world, which is to sacrifice ourselves for our fellow men . . . and not to be distracted from this even by the thought of the prize we shall receive. We are all alike, and this mother who speaks to Jesus is like all mothers: I am going to give you my sons, but in return what will you make of them? In their turn the young men seem true sons of their mother; it may even be that, through jealousy of the other apostles, they had put her up to making this request. Jesus always had a tender feeling for mothers. If our mother were to speak with him, the two apostles may have thought, Jesus would appoint us to who knows what high office. All this is human—we are all alike in this, with no exception, and the man who, in order to avoid blushing for shame, and in order to become, as he says, independent, rejects every kind of divine reward or punishment, is even more proud and foolish. He ends by removing the power of rewards and sanctions from God, and assigning it to himself. 'You will be like God'[1]—the eternal refrain! Whoever rejects God as his rewarder appoints himself as his own rewarder—a fine exchange! Only God can be our end, as God alone is our beginning and our propulsive power.

Jesus tells us very clearly and firmly how things stand. He came to redeem men, and he wants with him men who will assist him in his work, and with the same purpose. As for the future, it is insulting to distrust our Father and his

1. Genesis iii, 5.

generosity; he is the only one we can trust. In order to be with Jesus we must desire nothing else but to love our Father and our brothers, even till death. To live wholly for God and for our fellow men, to live, and if need be, to die: this is the Christian life.

As brothers of Jesus we are granted the same grace, as much as we can bear of it, and consequently the same glory. We are his brothers, and so share in his inheritance. But who can be serenely sure, without presumption, of inheriting his glory? How can we be confident even of being in a state of grace here below? We are certainly far from sure of final perseverance; we must always tremble for ourselves, weaklings prone to sin and full of malice.

Jesus became man, a man like the rest of us. He wanted to teach us, by his presence as a man among us, not to be afraid. Who was born in more wretched circumstances than he? He knew all kinds of suffering, and when dying he felt that not only the men for whom he died but even his Father had forsaken him.

This is our life, and our death; let us leave all thought of reward to our Father, and cast ourselves into the thick of the fray. The earth is a battlefield; let us join battle.

16

'*There was a rich man, who was clothed in purple and fine
linen, and who feasted sumptuously every day. And at his
gate lay a poor man named Lazarus, full of sores, who
desired to be fed with what fell from the rich man's table;
moreover the dogs came and licked his sores. The poor man
died and was carried by the angels to Abraham's bosom.*'
Luke xvi, 19–22

'...the dogs came'

This is an awesome detail, the references to the dogs who
were Lazarus' only companions and cared for him as best
they could, licking his ulcered flesh with their soft warm
tongues: a detail that strikes fear into our hearts. That poor
man was alone with God, and those dogs. There does not
seem to have been a man to take notice of him.

The sufferer has with him only God and brute nature,
that is, his own pain. Other men avoid him. Job was no better
off for company—the men who came to him came only to add
to his suffering. Our Lord died practically alone; his apostles
had fled; his disciples were no more; the few women who
stayed with his mother and John were kept at a distance and
only allowed to draw near at the moment of his death.

This solitariness is partly inherent in our nature. What
good can it do us to have a lot of people around when we
are suffering? What can they do for us? Sooner or later

the moment will come when even the doctors will no longer know what to do—they may not even know what ails us
—and we are in pain, perhaps dying. The loneliness of suffering, a loneliness to which we are constrained by the laws of
nature, is part of our destiny. In the most critical moments of
our lives we are alone, and no one can ever get near enough to
us to be able to enter into our lives and share them with us.
We find it difficult enough to enter into ourselves; the mystery
of our separate existences is not wholly revealed to us here
below.

In this state, which is melancholy and appears to us sometimes not only burdensome but unbearable, one would expect
to find sympathy, tenderness and the endeavour to surround
the sick man with all the best that can be offered, even if he
cannot be given all he requires. And this feeling is found in
warm-hearted people. We should be slandering our fellow
men if we tried to make out that all men are without compassion. But this is seen most commonly in the poorer folk, the
humble, those who have least of this world's goods. It is more
rarely seen in those who possess much of what the world
prizes: glory, power, beauty, wealth and skill. Everything
about them is rich, except their hearts. They have everything
else, except hearts, having lost these when they conquered
the world. Do not think I mean only the most brilliant men,
the exceptions; I am thinking rather of men of mediocre stature. A small fortune is enough to make a great egoist, and
no one is more vainglorious than the man who enjoys a small
share of glory. It would be easy to plot on the same graph a
man's progress in the good fortunes of this world, and his de-
cline in goodness—the same line which rises in one direction
drops in the other.

In order to find a remedy for this wretched state of affairs
God in his mercy wishes to strengthen and console our feeble
virtue by means of his precept of charity, and its correspon-
ding grace. We must ask the saints what charity is. In a word,
it is self-sacrifice, even to death, for our brothers; it is recognizing the Father as our own Father and loving him as such;
and recognizing men as our brothers, and loving them as

such; this is charity. Christianity says nothing else but this, demands nothing more.

It may be said that the Lord told this little parable before there was such a thing as Christianity; in fact, he told it in order to found the Christian society and so change the state of the world. After two thousand years of Christianity, has the world been changed?

Certainly Christianity has worked like leaven in men's hearts, and in the history of mankind, and continues so to work; but which of us would dare to say that this parable of our Lord's is merely a historical record, that there are no longer rich lords to burst with their own greed, and no more poor folk to die, literally, of hunger? But setting aside far-reaching historical considerations, what man would dare to say that the warning words of Jesus were not intended for him too? Can he boast that he enjoys no superfluity of wealth (we speak of superfluity, but anything more than the needful is almost always dangerous), and that everyone around him has all that he needs? And is not the gravity of our present situation enough to refute any presumptuous claim we might make that we are already good and dutiful Christians? If we wish to make an exact assessment of our failings as Christians, let us count whatever there is of superfluity in our possessions, and then count how many people there are around us who lack even the necessities of life. This is a means of reckoning that cannot fail.

17

*'There was a householder who planted a vine-yard, and set a
hedge around it, and dug a wine press in it, and built a tower,
and let it out to tenants, and went into another country. When
the season of fruit drew near, he sent his servants to the
tenants, to get his fruit, and the tenants took his servants and
beat one, killed another, and stoned another. Again he sent
other servants, more than the first; and they did the same to
them. Afterwards he sent his son to them, saying: "They will
respect my son." But when the tenants saw the son, they said
to themselves, "This is the heir: come, let us kill him and have
his inheritance." And they took him and cast him out of the
vineyard, and killed him.'*

Matthew xxi, 33–9

'Come, let us kill him and have his inheritance'

This is the everlasting temptation of men, from Cain on-
wards. It was thus that the devil tempted Eve. Killing in order
to steal, stealing in order to possess—so much of human warfare consists of this. What pleasure there is in possession,
and how long this joy may last, and what use it is, is a mystery. The days go by, and the years; a whole life passes away;
four shovelfuls of earth and no one will ever bother about me
again. The words which Jesus places on the lips of the murderers in this parable represent, in their extreme brevity and
brutality, a whole attitude of mind which is not proper to

murderers only, but which, given the necessary precautions
and the right temperament, applies also to us, the 'respectable'
people. If others could know our thoughts on all occasions
they would not be so fond of us as we are of ourselves. We
do not think highly of one another. We judge others by ourselves; for the sake of a quiet life we preserve a sort of mutual
respect which inevitably, in the unguarded moments of anger
or the cowardly impunity of slander, breaks down completely.
What is harder to understand is that we all, from highest to
lowest, think we are not only respectable but honourable folk.
It is only the saints who think of themselves as sinners, actual
or potential. It is said that when St Philip Neri met a murderer being taken to prison he ran his hands through his hair,
and raising his eyes to Heaven begged God to help him, help
him, Philip, capable of even more dreadful crimes. The saints
have always considered themselves unworthy, not so much
of the esteem of men as of the mercy of God.

But we have never killed anyone, we are incapable of killing
a fly. As far as flies are concerned, that may well be; and
yet we ought to remember that we take a delight in slaughter-
ing them when they torment us, and swatting one, two or
three with the fly whisk is a pleasant summer pastime. Nor
must we forget, although it is useless to dwell on this, that the
presence on our tables of meat and fish, without which it is
impossible to prepare a decent meal, presupposes dreadful
slaughter. People say it is horrible to live in the vicinity of a
slaughter house. So it does not look as if we were the angelic
creatures we claim to be: we also are carnivorous animals (un-
pleasant thought!).

So much for flies. As for not killing men, the less said the
better. For men to kill one another, however inconceivable
and inadmissible this may seem, has been an everyday occurrence in all ages, even in our own most fortunate and humani-
tarian era. We men even killed the Son of God, when he became man. We should never forget this, above all when we
fill our mouths with words like humanism, humanitarianism,
and so on.

But, we may insist, there are many worthy folk who would

never hurt a hair of anyone, and we ourselves, in all modesty, are among their number. Apart from natural goodness of heart, we are also Christians, and devout Christians. A mere dispute, let alone a crime, would fill us with horror. This seems true, and indeed is true. We have not said that we are all a gang of murderers, a band of brigands, an association of criminals. We have said that there are shades and degrees, ways and means . . . and we are not trying here to see what extremes may be reached, but from what seeds and roots the evil springs. The seeds and roots of violence are nourished within us; and perhaps they are no longer merely seeds and roots. Do we bear rancour, resentment or anger? Are we impatient, surly, bad-tempered? There are so many off-shoots, so many branches of the same evil tree. These books of cruel polemics, of pitiless satire, of horrible scorn and insidious corruption that we praise as inimitable masterpieces of our literature—what are they but 'flowers', if we may so call them, from the same evil stem? And are they not also flowers of evil, the many fortunes amassed at another's expense, the numerous careers advanced at the price of another's humiliation, the reputations swollen by a systematic denigration of rivals and competitors? We are always trying to make ourselves superior to other men; and we dare to reject as inexact and inapplicable to ourselves the Gospel's terrible words: 'Come, let us kill him, and have his inheritance.'

Well then, must we despair? Were those heretics right who asserted that man can have no other than an 'imputed' righteousness, that is, a mask of righteousness, and are those correct who maintain today that everything in us is a conflict of elements and instincts, and so good or evil cannot exist? The truth is that we *can* be wicked and, with the help of grace, we *can* and *must* be good. But we ought not to be so light-hearted about it, and so careless; we ought not to strut about so proudly, or recline at ease. Without speaking of divine justice, and we know how terrible it is to fall into the hands of the living God,[1] let us remember that our share of the mercy of God is measured by our feeling of need. And we should consider

1. cf. Hebrews x, 31.

ourselves guilty of our own sins and also guilty, out of a feeling of solidarity, of all men's sins.

The repentance preached by Jesus, and urged upon us by the Church during Lent, consists in our acknowledgment of sin, a necessary preliminary for our indispensable renewal.

18

'And he said, "There was a man who had two sons: and the younger of them said to his father, 'Father, give me the share of property that falls to me.' And he divided his living between them. Not many days later, the younger son gathered all he had and took his journey into a far country, and there he squandered his property in loose living. And when he had spent everything, a great famine arose in that country, and he began to be in want. So he went and joined himself to one of the citizens of that country, who sent him into his fields to feed swine. And he would gladly have fed on the pods that the swine ate, and no one gave him anything." '

Luke xv, 11–16

'He squandered his property'

He squandered his property, all he possessed, what he had, and what he was. He had nothing left; he envied the beasts in his charge, for they were fine, round and fat, and he was dying of hunger.

He squandered also his spiritual inheritance, utterly and completely. His love for God, for his father and his family, his upbringing and his friends, perhaps even his love for a woman and the hope of having sons—all this he threw away. It was certainly not with the idea of committing suicide that he broke so many sacred bonds, left his home and his father, and fled from his own land. Something must have lured him away. He was foolish but presumably not stupid; something must have dazzled his eyes. The hope of huge profits? passionate love for a woman? a mad desire for glory? Or, more simply, was it just a young man's impatience with an ordered and tranquil life, boredom with goodness, restlessness? We do not know, but it must have been something very serious because he dared to ask his father for his rightful share in the inheritance, and he obtained what he asked for. He set out, and in the act of leaving home he had already given up a great deal; he had renounced God, and his father and his home; he had renounced his education and way of life—and saying this is not a snobbish observation, but means that he had given up a life with a certain dignity like great music, or deep breathing, the rhythm of a wholesome way of life.

What he threw away later on is easy to imagine, even without the aid of hypotheses and deductions. He was foolish and sinful, but nevertheless there must have been some dream of good that lured him away from his own people. Well, he lost that dream too. He wanted glory, pleasure, absolute freedom, power; for these he forsook everyone and everything; no dream of his came true, everything failed him. It is easy to say this, but if we allow ourselves to imagine what bitter mouthfuls that wretched youth had to swallow we shudder. He must have been fairly rich, he was not lacking in courage and initiative, he may even have been highly intelligent— (which does not mean he could not be silly—on the contrary . . .); falling lower and lower in the social scale and ending up as a swineherd must have meant some dreadful humiliations! So much quarrelling and spite, instead of love! So much hardship and disgrace instead of ease and wealth! So much scorn and bloody defeat, instead of glory and power! In short, he gambled away even his dreams. He forfeited the life he wished to lead, after having forfeited the life he had led before.

We can imagine how his faculties and health had suffered. We know them well, these terrible squanderers. They become stupefied, miserable, vicious. They gamble away their youth, they are like bundles of dirty rags, so worn and ragged that we are afraid to wash them. At twenty-five they are sick old men, like worm-eaten wood, wet and rotten timber. They cannot reason or remember, they can hardly speak. Vice is a brutal master. To have been set to that particular job means he must have become almost like a beast himself; otherwise he could surely have found something better. And no one seems to have bothered much about him, for they left him without food. So he had squandered his whole existence, and now found himself on the brink of madness and death. It is easy to say this too: but whoever thinks of the terrible suffering these words imply cannot fail to weep. The prodigal son, as Jesus describes him to us, is as near to us as one of our own family, one of ourselves; to be precise, as near as every one of us is to himself. 'You are the man,'[1] we think, and the thought saddens us.

But as a general rule, in order to be free of conscience and remorse, we refuse to recognize ourselves in the portrait of the prodigal son. No, we say to ourselves, we haven't reached that point yet. Well, let us consider for a moment the notion of mortal sin, which in our careless way we leave very vague and abstract. The extent of our separation from God, when we have gravely offended him, is much greater than the distance between the prodigal son's home and the 'far' country where he ended up. And our state as sinners is no better than that of the prodigal who herded the swine and envied them their pods. The sinner encounters far worse things than this, and has far more sinful longings. The saints mourned even over venial sins. A single impulse of vanity terrified them. It is said of St. Alphonsus de' Liguori that once, in the middle of solemnly celebrating Pontifical Mass in his cathedral, at the moment when, according to the ritual, he was incensed immediately after the altar, he felt something like a stab of vanity, and was horrified to find himself for a moment in its power, wounded, a prisoner. A lie which in the light of our own days seems even worthy of admiration (we talk about a 'fine lie'), when seen in the light of God is a monstrous thing.

1. II Samuel xii, 7.

A pious and witty man once said that small animals claim more victims than do the larger beasts; not many of us die in a lion's jaws but many from the attacks of bacilli. Venial sins, if numerous and virulent, can waste our substance, no less than one grave sin.

19

'*When the unclean spirit has gone out of a man, he passes through water-less places seeking rest; and finding none he says, "I will return to my house from which I came." And when he comes he finds it swept and put in order. Then he goes and brings seven other spirits more evil than himself, and they enter and dwell there; and the last state of that man becomes worse than the first.*'

Luke xi, 24–6

'... and they enter and dwell there'

The first time a doctor showed me, under the microscope, all the living and harmful organisms which disport themselves in the blood of a victim of malaria, I was dismayed. I felt, not so much like a man as like a hotel. I seemed to have lost dignity, and human life was certainly seen to be much more precarious. We are preyed upon by so many creatures, not only around but inside us: living creatures, not inanimate things.

If there existed, as there exists for visible phenomena, a microscope by means of which we could examine every moral act, in its most secret component elements, I fear that we should see that our souls are infected no less than our bodies. If there are bacilli in our bodies, it is no laughing matter; it is still more grim if, as our Lord said, there are devils in our souls.

But, you will say, the Lord was speaking in parables, allegorically. And if there is a learned man, a rationalist, present, he will inform you also that in those days and in those countries psychological disorders were always supposed to be the work of devils, and people whom today we cure with a course of injections, or a brief stay in a nursing home, were thought to be maniacs. But we are not speaking of savage times and tropical jungles: it was the age of Virgil; Plato had died several centuries earlier. We dismiss past centuries too summarily, with a careless ignorance which will be evident in all its foolishness to our children and grandchildren. And, apart from these historical considerations, it would be well to consider that, devils or no devils, the fact of our wickedness, even if we refuse to call it sin, is still very grave, a problem not to be solved with the methods of 'thrillers' or by lay systems of morality. We have wrought our wickedness to such an exasperated pitch that a halt now seems imperative, if only for reflection.

.　　　.　　　.　　　.　　　.

We are busy creating scientific systems, social theories, and international schemes; we speak of brilliant progress made. Meanwhile the cruelty of man to other men has reached an apocalyptic frenzy and extension. It is not even necessary to refer to the tortures used in recent years: there must be others, that men dare not even mention; and more are probably held in reserve. We have got to the point of poisoning the soul, disintegrating the personality. We do not deny that in ancient times men were cruel, and expert in inflicting pain. We call them barbarous, uncivilized, primitive. But we, who are supposed to be civilized and progressive, are even worse. Is our wickedness also merely a psychological disorder? We would like to know the answer because the problem admits of no delay—we must find a solution. To go on like this means sinking more deeply every day in dirt and blood.

.　　　.　　　.　　　.　　　.

Sin which is unrecognized and unconfessed is like an infection that has not been diagnosed and dealt with: it invades the whole organism and destroys it. We refuse to admit that we are sinners—this is our guilt and our punishment. We shall never receive forgiveness, which alone heals us from sin and wipes it away, until we ask for it. The least we can do to obtain it is to ask for it, and it is so wonderful a thing that it can be had for the asking. No fairyland is more full of wonders than the kingdom of God.

But are there really devils inside us? And do they feel quite at home? The Christian doctrine about this is fairly explicit. First of all, devils exist. They are, moreover, spiritual beings, not bound to any corporeal form. They are enemies of God and our enemies too. They have an intelligence, and possess means, immeasurably superior to ours; but they cannot force our free will. Since God respects our free will, no one and nothing else can force it. But the devil can lay snares for it, and he is a past master of snares. Once granted this, it is easy to understand that a spirit can dwell in us, once he succeeds in acting in us and upon us. He may enter into the play of our thoughts and feelings, as best he can, with God's permission; he may even act on our bodily powers, our senses, our vital functions and limbs. For the devil to dwell in us it is enough for him to be able to act in us. And if he not only acts but, through our own cowardice, acts victoriously, with a sure touch, and quite confidently, we at once, like puppets, turn to him and religiously obey him—then naturally the devil makes himself at home in us, sets up his seat, perhaps even his headquarters. The Lord may have exaggerated just a little, speaking figuratively and dramatically, but, on the whole, what he said was only too exact, and devastatingly to the point.

.   .   .   .   .

And we, wretched fools as we are, we even have ourselves photographed in poses of love or glory, and preen ourselves in public or in our drawing-rooms, admiring our reflections in our mirrors as if we were towers of ivory, superior spirits, surpassing beauties, exceptional men and women. Oh, if we could but see who and what are at work around us, and inside us! We would be saved from Hell, because we should see it already here, in our souls.

20

'When they heard this, all in the Synagogue were filled with wrath. And they rose up and put him out of the city, and led him to the brow of the hill on which their city was built, that they might throw him down headlong. But passing through the midst of them he went away.'

Luke iv, 28–30

'. . . that they might throw him down headlong'

When we hear that the inhabitants of Nazareth, becoming ever more furious and resentful as they shouted and vociferated, reached the point of dragging Jesus to the brow of a hill in order to hurl him into the precipice below, we are alarmed, horrified and full of righteous anger. How stupid they were! how wicked! These people were from his own village, they must have been proud of him once; possibly our Lady still lived in the village. What beasts! What maddened beasts!

And we are right. These expressions of horror do us credit, this indignation shows the profound nobility of our feelings. But just think: do we really behave any better than the men of Nazareth, as individuals or as mankind *en masse*? When we look at ourselves closely, coolly, without batting an eyelid, we see very little to make us cheerful and haughty, and much to make us blush for shame.

It may be said that every century since the birth of Jesus

has witnessed some attempt to suppress him, perhaps even by throwing him into a ditch. The ditch has sometimes been heresy, or politics, or philosophy or revolution, sometimes scholarship and at other times ignorance—in fact there has been a bit of everything. Very often, during the centuries, we have seen Jesus dragged to his death by a furious shouting mob. Here we have only time to refer to two recent attempts, one made by philosophers and philologists, the other by social reformers. Today there are philosophies galore, all disagreeing with one another, except in denying Christ. They loathe each other and go their separate ways; but as soon as Jesus comes into sight and seems to be drawing nearer, they become reconciled with each other, find grounds for agreement, and begin to think of the best way to cast him down to his death, from the heights of 'thought'. There is a whole jungle of historical and philological sciences, united in the effort to 'deny' Jesus, as St John would say, deny his divinity and reduce him to our own wretched stature. The cliff from which they try to hurl him is philology. Others, the revolutionaries, lay their hands on him every day, drag him to the brink of the precipice, cast him down and give out that he is dead; and every time they have to do it all over again because the dead man never seems quite dead, and they have to try once more. The more they kill him the more he is alive.

Every century sees the repetition of disgusting scenes like this one in Nazareth, or even that of Calvary. Jesus comes towards us to save us; we go towards him to kill him: the story of every day and every age. Two thousand years have gone by since he was born for us, and we killed him; we continue to kill him and he continues to be born again.

Those were his enemies, we say. We are his friends, we are fond of him. It is true that no one ever was or is more loved than Jesus. We know of no human love stronger and more sublime than the love which men have felt for Jesus. There is no love story more enthralling than this story of the love with which men have responded to the Son of God's unbelievable love for them. No attachment to a native land, or to glory itself, ever reached the unbearable, glowing intensity of love which men's hearts have felt for Jesus. Of this we can be justly proud; it is our finest boast, and this alone would make it worth while to have been born men.

It is true we are not to be counted among his murderers; but are we sure we can be counted among his lovers? We are among those who would never stain their hands with murder, but nor would we risk staining them with blood by caring for a mortally wounded man; we go on our way horrified—even the thought of blood makes us shudder. So we always leave Jesus alone, in the hands of those who crucify him. While they are killing him we stay prudently at home, lest they should kill us too. Worse, we hardly dare admit it, but we are not only cowardly, not only terrified of being compromised, no, there is something that we are not afraid to do: we also insult Jesus, in our obscure mediocrity. We cast him out, without ceremony, without a spark of tenderness, from the height (if we can call it so) of the first temptation that comes our way. We cast Jesus out for the most inane and foolish vanities. And when in our hearts we hold a reception in honour of some passion, Jesus may knock at our door for ever: we leave him outside if he is outside, and if he is inside we throw him out. Out into the cold, the dark, the loveless night. Meanwhile, in the warmth and intimacy of our hearts, the siren music of earthly loves is heard and, as the unconfessable sins begin their dance, masked death enters on the arm of pleasure.

21

'If your brother sins against you, go and tell him his fault, between you and him alone. If he listens to you, you have gained your brother. But if he does not listen, take one or two others along with you, that every word may be confirmed by the evidence of two or three witnesses. If he refuses to listen to them, tell it to the Church, and if he refuses to listen even to the Church, let him be to you as a Gentile and a tax collector. Truly, I say to you, whatever you bind on earth shall be bound in Heaven, and whatever you loose on earth shall be loosed in Heaven.'

Matthew xvii, 15–18

'If he refuses to listen even to the Church . . .'

There are many people who never listen to the Church, either because they do not know her at all, or because they do not know her well, and so either do not wish to join her or have decided to leave her. But there are many, even among her own children, who do not listen to her—the same children who would be horrified at the mere thought of one day abandoning her, and would consider it a sin, a grave sin, not to marry sacramentally, not to baptize their children, or not to be buried with the rites of the Church. They neither listen to her nor defy her; sometimes they are hardly aware of her.

In times like ours, when we have experienced what one might almost call the omnipotence of every sort of association, cultural and criminal, political and recreational, this particular association we call the Catholic Church seems to enjoy no power at all. I do not mean power in the sense of her historical activity, but power in her own characteristic, exclusively spiritual domain. The fact that a certain man makes his communion for the sake of publicity, that is, for the same reason for which yesterday he abstained from communion, means that the Church today counts for something in the world, but a communion of this kind brings her no advantage: a man does not so easily become a faithful member of the Church. In fact, he really has less faith than an unbeliever. On the other hand, those who derive from such cases, which are fortunately rare, reasons for endless deprecations, insinuations and lamentations (it's all over with religion, they are all hypocrites, the Church is a den of thieves, the priests are now electioneering agents, etc., etc.) show themselves not friends but slanderers of truth. Most men let themselves be ruled and dragged along by popular fashion and popular opinion. It is not the Church's fault if today some people hide like insects in the folds and seams of her robes, whenever she enjoys power and prestige; nor is it her fault if so many of her children desert her in times of persecution and grave hardship.

.   .   .   .   .

It is another matter we must insist upon. The Christian has not yet understood what kind of life he must share in common, necessarily in common, with all other Christians, if he wants to be a true practising Catholic. Even in church, while all are listening to the same Mass, everyone is isolated, as if in a wilderness, reciting his private prayers. If we ask one of the faithful in which diocese he was born he may not even know what a diocese is. The same may be said of the parish. And when we leave these simple ecclesiastical terms to speak of far more important notions, of a much graver necessity, for example, the doctrine of the communion of saints, the answers we should receive, if any, would horrify us. It is no excuse to say that we live the Catholic life, as we live our physical life, instinctively, unconsciously, without looking at ourselves in the mirror, with a natural acquiescence. The Catholic life is essentially a life of knowledge and love, knowledge and love of the Father, knowledge and love of our fellow men; but there can be no knowledge, and no love, of what is unknown. It is impossible to be Christians without knowing it—that would be too easy.

Being of one mind with the Church, having what our forefathers used to call by its Latin name the *sensus Ecclesiae*, dwindles every day among us and in us, unless we nourish it by sharing the life of the Church. To do this it is necessary that we should place her before any other association, and know what is our parish, what is our diocese, who are our shepherds and our fellow sheep in the flock and fold. We must form a true spiritual unity, one family. The sick of the parish should be thought of as our own sick. We ought to know exactly which parishioners no longer receive Holy Communion. All the children of the parish should meet. The parish priest should be the connecting link, precisely because he is charged with the spiritual rule of his flock, with preaching and the celebration of Holy Mass, with Holy Communion and the Sacraments.

In the same way, the faithful of a diocese should all know each other, and recognize each other even at the ends of the earth, if they should travel so far. Then a bishop may truly be said to possess his diocese, when the faithful are no longer blocks of stone heaped together, but form a building, a house of God.

·　　　·　　　·　　　·　　　·

There are some problems, and the gravest of all, which cannot be solved unless we listen to the Church, as Jesus tells us to do. All our dealings with God, and the best of our dealings with men, pass through the Church and begin and end there. We must not attach too much importance to forms of life which are born and die in time. Even if they seem to flourish they are short-lived because temporal; we must set store by those forms which were born with Christianity and will last as long as it survives. To be modern minded is all very well, up to a certain point. For the last two thousand years the Christian world has been divided into dioceses, and this is a source of wonder to students of history, but we Christians know nothing about this, or if we know, it means nothing to us.

22

'And he called the people to him and said to them, "Hear and understand: not what goes into the mouth defiles a man, but what comes out of the mouth, this defiles a man." Then the disciples came and said to him, "Do you know that the Pharisees were offended when they heard this saying?" He answered, "Every plant which my Heavenly Father has not planted will be rooted up." '

Matthew xv, 10–13

'Every plant which my Heavenly Father has not planted will be rooted up'

Even the most deeply rooted, bold and fearless unbeliever cannot help occasionally wondering why it is that in the last 2000 years Europe has seen such a succession of civilizations, dynasties, kingdoms and institutions, whereas Christianity still remains in its place, and gives no apparent signs of being willing to leave it to others. People frequently point to a similar survival in the case of Islam and Buddhism, and the religion of the Chinese—but this parallel is not exact, or exact only in part.

Europe has been renewing herself with a speed and thoroughness found nowhere else. Her heart-searchings have been continual and essential; there have been revolutions in thought, in political forms, in arts and languages, in everything but religion. A historical demonstration of this would make a most interesting book, but the believer does not need it and the unbeliever would take good care not to read it, lest he should find himself compromised and perturbed. All the vineyards which the Father in Heaven did not plant—'my Father is a vinedresser' said Jesus[1] in another context—all the vineyards which are not of his planting are in the end uprooted; the tree that was born from the smallest of all seeds —another saying of Jesus[2]—suffers the wear and tear of the seasons, but does not die.

Merely to remember the immensity and violence of events which we have seen with our own eyes in recent years brings back the thought of all the glory and misery that have followed each other, the one generally giving rise to the other.

Gigantic fortunes lost in gigantic disasters; enormous wealth disappearing suddenly from sight, together with its owner, into yawning chasms; power which no one could resist or confute fading as our dreams fade on waking; invincible forces which had reached the peaks of the maddest and most furious violence, broken, reduced to dust, and like dust blown away on the wind. The story of men on this earth has the splendours and shadows of a day; radiance so bright that it seems eternal, darkness as black as Hell—and all this in the space of a few hours is scattered, melts and disappears without a trace, and its whereabouts is unknown. The Church founded by Jesus, which to the eyes of the world seems likewise composed of merely earthly elements, plays her part in the blood-stained vintage and the all-destroying harvests of time, and yet never disappears, as all other forces disappear, but remains with us. That one bunch of grapes is never gathered, that ear of corn is never reaped. When shall we at last understand that the Church is alive with a more than human life, one that is superhuman indeed, and truly divine? Many men have sought desperately for something for their fellow men that might be more than human—and they have always beaten and broken their heads against the iron barriers, the boundaries of humanity. Yet the meanest, roughest,

1. John xv, 1.
2. cf. Mark iv, 31.

poorest Christian—if he is really a Christian—is far more than a man, far more and better than a so-called great man, greater than the greatest of men. Tales have been told of the Superman, and for the sake of this tragic fable men have lost their souls; but the Christian is no creature of fable, he is truly a man who is more than a man. Only in the Christian is mankind redeemed and saved; and when man is redeemed he crosses the frontiers of the divine world; once more he is an adopted child of God, and shares in God's life.

But we must point out that in the Church herself all is not fixed and immutable. What the Father planted cannot be moved, but what men have planted is not immoveable. The Jews gloried in the stones of the Temple and today we have good reason to reproach them for this—but what do we ourselves glory in? So often even good Christians are allured by earthly grandeur, and worldly pomp, by power and its echo, glory! How often their pride in the beauty of their faith rests on the majesty of its ceremonial, the massed numbers of the faithful, the trappings, the festivities and the clamour! So often the more cultured and serious-minded are proud of the profound thought, the splendid artistic achievements, the variety and exuberance of Christian civilization! Not that these beauties are to be despised and considered of no account: they are indeed the natural consequences of that primary essential beauty which consists principally in the knowledge and love of the Father, and the knowledge and love of our fellow men, the beauty of that first vineyard which the Father planted and which will never be uprooted, like all those others which appear and disappear according to the seasons. St Joseph Benedict Labre on his pallet bed was no less great than St Louis IX on his throne: fine Christians, both of them, although so differently attired and equally poor in all that this world prizes, and equally rich in what is precious in the eyes of God. Their true glory is their holiness. We leave it to poets to extol their thrones and their lice (if lice have their poets too); holiness is something else.

The same thing happens in every one of us. Let us take care not to run after the clamour of this world, but to recollect ourselves in the silence of God. We must not get over excited about vineyards which we, or others like ourselves, have planted, but think rather of God's vineyard. To know and love God, to know and love our fellow men, to know and love Jesus, the Man God, our only Mediator: this is what we must do, and in the way which God has entrusted to the Church. We must not confuse the Word of God, which alone gives life and death, with the words of men; nor must we over-lay divine tradition in the Church with those traditions which are only human, and just because they are only human must not be allowed to take precedence over those of God and his Church. We are so keen on rushing here and there setting up organizations of all kinds—but God requires only one kind of activity from us, that of 'doing good'. And this is the only work that no one is willing to do. We don't like 'doing good'; it means a great effort, nobody will notice it—but this is just as it should be. To do our duty well requires more Christian virtue than doing what we piously and pompously describe as 'good works'. The best way of doing good to others is to be good ourselves. Social reforms, cultural societies, political associations, Assistance Boards—what a fervour of activity all round us! And yet the only activity God requires of us is just being good and doing good—and this is what nobody wants to understand.

23

'Now when the sun was setting, all those who had any that were sick with divers diseases brought them to him, and he laid his hands on every one of them and healed them. ... And when it was day he departed and went into a lonely place.'

Luke iv, 40–2

'... he departed and went into a lonely place'

Jesus was the only man who did not need to recollect himself in prayer in order to find God, the only man who did not need to draw apart from his fellows and be to some extent detached even from himself, in order to find that silence in which alone we hear the voice of God. He was Jesus; he had God with him, joined in the unity of one Person; and yet from time to time he fled to some out-of-the-way and lonely place, in order to be alone with God. And we, stunned by the clamour of the world, the confusion of men, and the contradictory variety of our many interior voices, we never make up our minds to create a little solitude around us and within; it is almost as if we felt an aversion, a physical aversion, to solitude. Alone, we are like children in the dark. As for the company of our Heavenly Father, either we do not know what it is, or we are afraid of it, as Adam was afraid after he had sinned. The presence of sin cannot bear the presence of God; we can have one or the other, but not both.

If a man is not afraid of solitude it means he is on good terms with God. The better the terms the more genuine and profound is his love of solitude. For the Lord does not speak in the storm;[1] the mercy of God steals into the heart that is at peace. The anger of God, instead, is terrible: the foundations of the earth tremble at his passing. To avoid his wrath we can take refuge only in his mercy; we must flee from the tumult of the world, make a cell of our own hearts and invite the Lord to dwell therein with us so that we may listen to his voice, and see him face to face.

For this purpose it is not necessary to make fantastic plans of seeking out some inaccessible retreat, some inviolable cave in the mountains, or the seclusion of a monastery. Those who indulge in such projects, pleading their love of solitude, do so in order to be able to find an excuse for not putting themselves to the test, so that they can say their schemes were found impracticable. What a terribly destructive whirlpool life is! they say, and my work!—if you could only see what I have to do! I never have a moment's respite. I wake with my head already caught in the machinery of the day's engagements; at night I can hardly sleep. But it's my duty, believe me, a social obligation. So many people need me, and I must not, indeed I will not, send them away unsatisfied. If you knew how much good one does, and even that is not enough! One would need forty-eight hours every day, not a paltry twenty-four.

This is what they say. I say this too. We all do. It is our way of complaining about our difficulties, but there is more than a note of vainglory in it. We do so much good that we are worn out, literally exhausted. And what about God? Has God no part in all our doing and speaking and receiving and visiting? Does God need nothing from us? Just suppose he does need us—not this or that activity of ours, but ourselves, our souls, our tranquil minds, one moment of conversation with him, one glance from us? Would it not be possible to make an appointment with God for a quarter of an hour, or ten minutes, or even five? Let us think for a moment. When

1. I Kings xix, 11.

A.G.&G.—F

death comes, what will remain of our work? Do we really believe that when we have died the world will find it hard to carry on without us? Or have to slow down, perhaps? After our death what will be left? Do you believe that what you have done will remain? You are mistaken, it will not remain—it will disappear in its turn, in a flash, as you have disappeared. And even if it were to remain, it would not remain for you but for those who are still in the world, as long as they are here. What will remain for you of your work is not what you have done, but how you have done it. Whether you did it well or ill, this will remain—nothing else—whether you were an emperor or a chimney sweep, a brilliant inventor or mentally deficient, does not matter. It is not what you have done that will matter to God, and therefore to your soul, but how you have done it, well or ill. Our actions will not be judged by their success but by the spirit we have put into them.

.   .   .   .   .

You may say that this way of reasoning plays into the hands of the slothful, and does away with any reward or incentive for work. If in the eyes of God Michelangelo counts for no more and no better than any breaker of stones, what is all this leading up to? Pure fanaticism? The negation of civilization, art, politics, etc., etc.? It is leading up to God and Paradise, nowhere else. If Michelangelo was born Michelangelo, he will be no less Michelangelo if he lives for God than he would be if he lived only for himself and his glory; in fact, he will be himself in a nobler and more perfect degree. Michelangelo himself was grieving when he wrote: 'The fables of this world have robbed me of time given for the contemplation of God.' What makes man great in the sight of God and eternity is not his genius but his goodness. Goodness belongs, or may belong, to everyone, while genius is the lot of few. In fact, genius, great genius, is an accidental, while goodness is the substance.

Every now and then at least let us draw apart to talk with God, to be alone with him. With so many artificial lights around us we have given up looking at the sky to see it full of stars. The myriad voices we hear prevent us from hearing the voice of God. We never receive our soul, to enquire about her health and her needs. She may be sick and we never visit her; or poor, without even the necessities of life, and we do not go to her aid. And so very firmly, even if with an absent-minded air, we shut our door against God.

24

'*He had to pass through Samaria. So he came to a city of Samaria, called Sychar, near the field that Jacob gave to his son Joseph. Jacob's well was there, and so Jesus, wearied as he was with his journey, sat down beside the well. It was about the sixth hour.*'

John iv, 5–6

'Jesus, wearied as he was with his journey, sat down beside the well'

This is a small detail, but a very moving one. The author of the *Dies Irae* had noticed this too, and for that solemn hour when our poor flesh, now cold, lies like a dead weight in the church aisle, with four lit candles around it and the mourning of the few who loved us, he has dared to suggest we should remind the Lord of this: *Quaerens me, sedisti lassus*. We can imagine Jesus, covered with the dust of the road, exhausted, pausing to rest by the side of a well, lonely and pensive.

Some poets have seen in his search for us a sort of divine pursuit, and the symbolism of a chase, already to be found in the Bible, is traditional in all spiritual literature. But we do not need this beautiful but alien imagery, or any other symbolic figure; the truth is beautiful in itself and for itself, just as it is. Jesus has walked along our roads. He knows their toilsomeness and their charm. He has trodden them in the sun, in rain, at night, alone, with a few companions, with

many, speaking, keeping long silences—with the eagerness
of departure and the melancholy of return. He knows their
unbearable length, roughness and danger. From his own experience he knows all about the fine wide roads which slope
gently downwards, full of shade and pleasant resting places,
with grand views at every turn. And he knows also the stony
paths, narrow, overgrown with briars, that wind up the hill-
side, full of elbow bends and fearful precipices and dangers.
From these roads he drew his imagery to describe the way to
Hell and the way to Paradise.

A road is a mysterious thing even in the humility of its purpose. It serves as a link between men, and this function of a
road must have been pleasing to Jesus. In fact, he did not
hesitate to compare it once to himself. He said in so many
words: I am the way. Not a way but *the* way. There is never
more than one road, when it is a good one, and the straighter
it is the better.

What sort of roads are ours, the roads we tread from
morning till night? Whither do they lead us? Merely by considering the roads we take we can get an idea of the direction
in which we are going, the direction of our lives. Where are
we going? And where do we wish to go? The reply to these
questions tells us what we are and what we do. There is no
escape from this, the roads we take form the net in which we
are caught.

Meanwhile, the path leading to the church is almost always
overgrown with grass. We go this way once every Sunday,
wearing our best Sunday shoes. It is not a well-trodden way.
It may seem very strange, but it is a fact that churches are
almost always on hill-tops, and we have to climb up to them.
There are very few valley shrines, almost all are built on the
summits of mountains, or halfway up. There is a reason for
saying that a person who is getting steadily worse is going
downhill. And when we speak of an ambitious man we say
he is rising higher and higher. Height is synonymous with
goodness and depth with wickedness. And what of our roads?
Are they ascending or descending? Alas! perhaps it is not so
much a descent as a headlong fall. We let ourselves slip down

to the dark void of eternal damnation, at the slightest provocation, the most trivial temptation.

When we begin to pray we think we ought to be able at once to reach the most etherial heights, as if we could soar through the air. We do not understand that in order to go to God we have to climb, and climb a steep road, not at all easy or convenient. There are Christians who refuse to submit to the most elementary training or the lightest discipline, and to hear them speak one would think they had reached the highest regions of prayer, of the mystic state, of St John of the Cross.

They have never succeeded in saying a whole Our Father, from beginning to end, without the interruptions of frivolous thoughts and foolish distractions, and yet they prate about the Dark Night and the Prayer of Quiet. What lucky people! How do they manage it? Are they not perhaps victims of their own imagination? of their, dare we say, slothful nature? When we are reluctant to move we stay at the foot of the slope, lost in meditation, as if to cover up our spineless indolence. As a general rule, those who reach the mountain peaks do not speak of them, and those who speak of them have never seen them. Mountaineers and Alpinists are the least talkative people we know and, understandably, the most chary of dramatic gestures: one cannot strike an attitude when clinging to the ridge of a mountain summit. It is easier to strike attitudes on the wide flat road which slopes imperceptibly downwards: the road to Hell.

25

'*Early in the morning he came again to the temple; all the people came to him, and he sat down and taught them. The scribes and the Pharisees brought a woman who had been caught in adultery, and placing her in the midst they said to him, "Teacher, this woman has been caught in the act of adultery. Now in the law Moses commanded us to stone such. What do you say about her?" This they said to test him, that they might have some charge to bring against him. . . . He stood up and said to them, "Let him who is without sin among you be the first to throw a stone at her." And once more he bent down and wrote with his finger on the ground. But when they heard it, they went away, one by one, beginning with the eldest, and Jesus was left alone with the woman standing before him. Jesus looked up and said to her, "Woman, where are they? Has no one condemned you?" She said, "No one, Lord." And Jesus said, "Neither do I condemn you; go, and do not sin again."* '

John viii, 2–11

'What do you say . . . ?'

So they actually dared to put such a question to Jesus! Strict guardians of the law, but without even a shred of inner life and feeling to enable them to perceive how often they themselves had transgressed!

In the act of administering justice they showed such unjust minds that we are surprised that their words did not burn their lips, and that they were able to utter them with such fierce and defamatory impudence. They told Jesus they knew . . . they wanted . . . they considered . . . they believed . . . they felt they ought to . . . and then they asked him what he thought about it—as if it were an academic discussion!

We also may be called upon to undertake the onerous and fearful duty of administering justice, but this does not in itself make us just; we ought to be just in order to do this. Not that perfect individual righteousness is necessary to make a good judge; a man can be an impartial and infallible judge and yet himself be a cesspit of vice. This happens very rarely, but it may happen, and such a man can be tolerated. It would instead be intolerable if a judge, himself an evil-doer, dared to inveigh against the criminal with expressions of scorn, malice and hatred, and this in the presence of God, with the crucified Christ silent on the wall behind him. Only those who are familiar with the sacrament of penance know how forgiveness makes brothers of us all. We all have the same need of God's forgiveness, and a man who does not feel this need is unworthy of it. A brother who sins is very much our brother, even for this reason alone.

Jesus is silent, but his silence is dismaying. If we think of it for a moment, it weighs heavily upon us. He does not speak, because he has come not to judge but to save. He does not summon us to the judgment throne but calls us to the mercy seat. He does not have us brought into his presence, he runs after us as we flee. He is silent, not because he does not know all about us, but because he wants to hear it from us, and he speaks only of repentance, of a conversion, a return—not wishing to concern himself with anything else. And can we men, called to administer social justice (and God wishes us to do this, as an exercise in charity), dare to assume an air of cruel disdain towards our brothers, and treat them, when condemned to expiate their crime, with such proud and merciless severity?

It is but rarely that we are assigned the explicit duty of judging our fellows. To make up for this we are always appointing ourselves as judges, accusers and judges at the same time. We think and speak of our neighbour with the greatest diffidence and reserve, when we are feeling kindly towards him; at other times with a thousand accusations, judgments and condemnations. Not one of his weaknesses escapes us; and if one of them should need a magnifying glass to be discerned, we take a delight in magnifying it beyond all recognition, projecting it on to a screen and holding forth about it. That is why we love and enjoy caricature so much; it depicts our neighbour as we like to think of him. That makes us laugh, makes us merry.

There was only one man who knew the truth about us all, and that man was Jesus. And he was silent, and called us all to come and be forgiven. He forgave all who asked for forgiveness, and prayed that those who did not ask for it should be forgiven too. Very seldom was his voice raised in condemnation, to scare the wolves and warn the sheep. We spend our time crying out, reporting, whispering, rebuking, lamenting; and we are no better than our fellows.

You may object that the Church herself respects and even commands both an exterior and an interior judgment seat, and keeps them quite separate from one another; why then should she wish us to return to public penance, and the obligatory examination of conscience? But who are those who ask this question? For one thing, there is no need of public confession. If there is one thing that cannot be kept hidden it is sin. Good deeds may escape men's notice, but not evil deeds. If evil is not confessed in its exact proportions men will think it is much graver and greater than it really is. In judging evil-doers we never sin by default, but always by excess. We are always hearing unbelievable horrors about people; we recount them and listen to them with angelic impassivity, as if they did not matter. Jesus, who never spoke ill of anyone, died the victim, first and foremost, of slander—and no one had done more good than he, and he was the only man to whom no one could impute a breath of sin, or taint of evil. He was silent even about those who were not silent about him, and dragged him to his death in a snare of calumnies and murderous accusations.

The silence of Jesus is a tremendous thing. It implies not absence, but a most awe-inspiring presence.

26

'*Jesus went up into the hills, and there sat down with his disciples. Now the Passover, the feast of the Jews, was at hand. Lifting up his eyes then, and seeing that a multitude was coming to him, Jesus said to Philip, "How are we to buy bread, so that these people may eat?" This he said to test him, for he himself knew what he would do. Philip answered him, "Two hundred denarii would not buy enough bread for each of them to get a little." One of his disciples, Andrew, Simon Peter's brother, said to him, "There is a lad here who has five barley loaves and two fish; but what are they among so many?" Jesus said, "Make the people sit down." Now there was much grass in the place; so the men sat down, in number about five thousand. Jesus then took the loaves, and when he had given thanks, he distributed them to those who were seated; so also the fish, as much as they wanted. And when they had eaten their fill, he told his disciples, "Gather up the fragments left over, that nothing may be lost." So they gathered them up and filled twelve baskets. . . .'*

John vi, 3–13

'... but what are they among so many?'

We anxiously ask ourselves the same question in almost the same words every time we try to do a good deed: we cannot do everything, we cannot help everyone. The fact is, we do hardly anything, and no one takes any notice of us. Our first impression when we try to behave well and do our duty is a feeling of solitude, almost like a fear of the void. When we are doing wrong all the machinery sets itself in motion and the wheels interlock precisely and rapidly, with a most beautiful ordered harmony: the man who makes money makes more and more; the ambitious man climbs higher and higher; the sensualist finds opportunities, so to speak, at every street corner. Instead, when we want to repent all our spiritual machinery grinds to a halt, and we ourselves are shunned like the plague. If we wish to be absorbed in prayer distractions spring up on all sides; and if we want to devote ourselves to the service of our neighbour everything goes awry, we get into all sorts of trouble, meeting with obstacles, disillusionment, bitterness, and even insults and punishments. To do wrong is so much easier than to do right; indeed it seems to require no effort on our part, merely inertia.

Besides the initial difficulties arising from our nature, prone to evil because wounded and weakened by original sin, there is another obstacle which derives, as it were, from the essential goodness of our nature. When we do wrong, the evil we do satisfies our passion and placates it, and we are soon content (if we are ever content . . .); instead, when we do good we are never satisfied. Goodness is infinite, like God; the more we do the more there is to do, and we never get it done. Goodness means a very great, unflagging effort. Hence the disappointment we always feel when we have done something good.

But we should be fools indeed if we accepted this disappointment as a discouragement, if we really allowed it to dishearten and dissuade us. It must rather serve as an incentive, increasing our zeal and our humility. The road of life is long— well, all the better! We shall follow it until the very hour in which God will call us; we shall follow it at a good, steady pace, sometimes running when need arises and at times even flying. . . . 'He rides easily who is carried by the grace of God.'[1] The most famous steeds and chargers of the epics of chivalry, and the winged Pegasus of antiquity, are as nothing

1. *Imitation of Christ.*

compared with the grace of God when this grace carries us to
our work and to our battles. Even the sense of our own limitations and insufficiency must urge us impatiently on; the very
length of the road makes us hurry, reluctant to pause, yet
riding cautiously lest we fall.

It would then be wrong to lose heart and despair, but it
would be no less wrong to indulge in the opposite excess. To
attempt too much is to fail. To undertake a task far beyond
our power means we are more anxious for renown than for
good results. We must have the courage to acknowledge our
limitations, and if we are asked to do more than we can we
must frankly admit that the task is too difficult and beyond
our capacity. If we wish to achieve that perfection which God
requires of us, we must have the strength of mind to do only
what we know we can do. It is extraordinary how blind we are
about this. If we are asked to bear a burden too heavy for our
shoulders we say at once that we cannot do this. But if we
are asked to take over a function or an office, it never seems
too much: we can do everything, our capacity is infinite. However onerous the work we are not afraid of being crushed by
it. But we must not be ruled by ambition if we want to do
what we were born to do. It is a different matter when we
are told to do something under obedience; the obedience
comes from God. God can draw blood from turnips, so when
it is his voice that calls us we have no need to tremble for our
insufficiency. But if it is ambition that calls, then we are in a
sad plight: it is once more the fable of the ox and the frog.

Between these two tempters, cowardice and foolhardiness,
both to be avoided, runs the brave man's road, our road. Not
to do less than our duty, and not to do more: this is the
king's highway. We can fail to do our duty by doing too little,
just as we can fail by doing too much. We can fail to perform
our allotted task by erring on the one side or on the other,
stray from the right road to the right or to the left. The urge
to do more may at the time seem to us holy zeal, or perhaps
even a call to heroism. Remember that the best is inimical
to the good. Let us stay on the high road of duty—that is our
safest course.

When, in the midst of our tasks, we begin to worry about not finding time to complete this or that good work, and to think that the world needs something else rather than a document we are annotating, an article we are writing, or some work in which we are engaged, we must not lose heart for so little, and above all we must not abandon our post, or our work. Jesus became man, that is, he also, God and Son of God, confined himself within our limits of time, space and number. Moreover, if every one of us, without exception, were to do his duty, the world would no longer be the world, it would be Paradise.

Trying to do too much, we always end by doing less than we should: the great sin of this century in fact consists in the invincible urge—we call it 'Titanism'—to exceed our own limitations, with the fine result, a result which is neither chimerical nor apocalyptic but a reality of yesterday, today and (God forbid!) tomorrow, that we end by destroying ourselves and others.

27

'The Passover of the Jews was at hand, and Jesus went up to Jerusalem. In the temple he found those who were selling oxen and sheep and pigeons, and the money-changers at their business. And making a whip of cords, he drove them all, with the sheep and oxen, out of the temple; and he poured out the coins of the money-changers and overturned their tables. And he told those who sold the pigeons, "Take these things away; you shall not make my Father's house a house of trade." His disciples remembered that it was written, "Zeal for thy house will consume me." '

John ii, 13–17

'His disciples remembered . . .'

When everything had already happened, and the prophecies had been fulfilled, his disciples remembered that the Lord had foretold precisely this. We do just the same: we remember God's law the moment after sinning against it. Adam became aware of his disastrous error when it was beyond repair. Every one of us is an Adam in his own way: we are all Adam by turns. We are always saying: I said so! If only I had followed my intuition! If only I had listened! If only I had thought better of it! We are always wise after the event. The damned and the souls in Purgatory were ruined by this wisdom after the event. We thought, they say, that it was mad-

95

ness to live a good life, but now we see that we were the mad-
men, truly and incurably mad.[1]

To avoid bitter surprises and vain lamentations there is
only one thing we can do: think first. And do not say this
advice is unnecessary. Is it true or not that it is useless to be
wise after the event? Well then, it is better to be wise first—
and this is good advice. Our fault lies just here, that we do
not make use of the simplest remedies, those nearest to hand.
We go on looking for rare and choice medicines when a
greater and better control over ourselves would protect us
much more effectively from some of our ailments. We invent
fantastic machines when it would be enough for us to watch
our step. To think first means living with such a Christian
mind and heart that the first glimpse of sin would dismay us.
Instead, we stumble into it without ever having looked it in
the face. Goodness! we say when this happens, is that what
sin looks like?

To think first means being on habitually affectionate, rev-
erent and humble terms with God. Certainly we cannot claim
that by merely attending Sunday Mass, and that probably
with scant attention, our soul is set on its guard against evil,
ready to spurn it at once and effectively. Nor can we claim
that by thinking of God barely five minutes a day we shall
be spiritually safeguarded from evil and enabled to resist it.
Evil is all around us, continually at work, manifold and immeasurable. However attentive we are we can never hope to
avoid it completely; that is why the Lord has given us the
wonderful prayer: lead us not into temptation but deliver us
from evil.[2] How do we think about God? What is our attitude to eternity? What do we feel about our own soul and
the souls of our fellow men? Are we ever concerned, seriously concerned, about a spiritual danger? Do we ever
pause to reflect and ponder, so as to make a truly Christian
decision?

We are infinitely careless and unforgivably rash. We vie
with one another—to ruin one another; we assist our brother

1. cf. Wisdom v, 4.
2. Matthew vi, 13.

men to go downhill, even sometimes pushing them over the precipice. We really give the impression that the Christian life does not exist for us, except in its exterior, domestic or social aspects. On the same day we go to Mass in the morning, and to an immoral entertainment in the evening: how can these two things be reconciled?

In the eighteenth century there was once an Abbot, a great wine-bibber, of whom it was said that in the morning he said Mass, and in the evening no one knew what he was saying. The same thing is true of us, for we rise from our prayers before they have worked like leaven in our souls. This is what thinking first means: it means leading a Christian life, humble, obedient, attentive, God-fearing.

The saints were never sure of themselves, and they were saints! We go on our way with terrifying insolence and boldness. Dangers? What are dangers to us? We have plenty of courage. We despise money, we feel no craving for it. Ambition is the vice of the mediocre—we abhor it. Vanity is for women: we men, we Christians, we this and that. . . .

And with all these fine sentiments we are more mangy than an old donkey, more dirty than a henhouse perch. We exhale worldliness through all our pores, like decaying bodies which emit a pestilential stench.

So we must be wise before the event. Our lives must be thoughtful, affectionate, in a word, devout, lived in the light and warmth of God.

28

'Jesus answered them, "I did one deed, and you all marvel at it. Moses gave you circumcision (not that it is from Moses, but from the fathers), and you circumcise a man upon the sabbath. If on the sabbath a man receives circumcision, so that the law of Moses may not be broken, are you angry with me because on the sabbath I made a man's whole body well? Do not judge by appearances, but judge with right judgment." '

John vii, 21–4

'... judge with right judgment'

As is well known, judgment is in itself that act of the intelligence with which we affirm or deny the existence of a property or quality or, if we can, the essence of a given subject. When we know something we begin to find out something to say about it, and this second degree of knowledge is called judgment. From a sequence of judgments we form a considered opinion. We repeat these elementary notions, these rudiments of philosophy, certainly not in order to show off our profound scholarship, but in order to lead up to reflections of a moral, or better, of a spiritual order. The first judgment that we must try to proffer correctly is in fact one which appears to be purely logical, and even quite extraneous to moral considerations. In itself and for itself the assertion that $2 \times 2 = 4$ does not seem to involve any ethical standard, but is simply a question of elementary arithmetic. If, however, my interest is no longer abstract, if this very simple addition involves some gain or loss to me personally, then the tiny distinct figures begin to dance before my eyes, and my sums no longer come right.

Not only the thief but also, and above all, the profiteer and speculator are said to do their accounts in their own way. And this is the lion's way: this is mine for this reason, that is mine for that reason, all is mine because I want it all. And so even arithmetic becomes a matter of opinion, and possibly involves a judgment, according to which 2×2 no longer invariably makes 4; it may be twisted to make something else. The passion of greed is a fire that melts even the most iron truths, and reduces the hardest stones to powder. The other passions, sensual or ambitious, develop no less heat, and are no less injurious. Our soul, given over to passion, is like a house on fire.

.   .   .   .   .

When our Lord said that the pure in heart would see God his words might be taken as the conclusion of what we have been saying. He has spoken the last word. It is indeed true that a pure heart, in spite of the fact that philosophers do not count it among the primary requirements for intellectual understanding, adds incredibly to the brightness and perceptiveness of the mind. Just as physical indulgence darkens and dims the eyes, so passion affects the capacity of those spiritual forces in us, our understanding and will; it dims their lustre, impedes and clogs their operation and deflects their aim.

Most of us will have known people, to all appearance rough and uncultivated, who, because they were so near to God, could reply with wonderful truth to the most delicate questions about God and the soul, and the divine life of the spirit. As long as I live I shall always remember, as one of the noblest things I have ever seen, how the face of a blind man lit up when he spoke to me of God. A blind man, remember. Yet there was in his face a transparency of light, a radiance of joy, that seemed to well up like a spring of pure water, wonderful to see. He did not say much, made no long speeches. He answered briefly, almost jestingly, as if he were amused by my questions. I had a clear impression that in me the steel blade of knowledge was cold and inert, while in him it burned red-hot, bright and glowing. What a miracle a pure heart is, and how humble and yet sublime its power of vision!

.   .   .   .   .

We find it difficult to believe that merely by loving God we can change our whole way of life and no longer be like those dull, fat, inert, obscure creatures which tremble and sting when they are touched. There begins in us a mysterious transformation by which the intelligence, the will, the senses, even the dull flesh itself, are still the same and yet 'with a difference'. We see what we never saw before, we do what we would never have done, our body comes to the aid of our soul. This is the work of grace, and if we do not check it, we shall be constantly renewed, like a plant in the spring. Grace is the beginning of divine life.

Saying this, we might be tempted to think that Heaven may be already within our grasp. But grace is given for the battle, glory for the victory. Grace is a weapon, glory a crown. It may happen, and frequently, and to no one more frequently than to those who are already advanced in the way of the Lord, that terrible battles have to be fought in total darkness, powerlessness and bewilderment. The Enemy may poison the water we drink, the bread we eat, the light of our eyes, our holiest affections. He may strike us down, as he struck Job. And yet we shall continue to judge rightly, even in the horror of the battle, amid the shrieks and groans. This happened to Job, who lost all but never lost himself, or God, because he never lost his right judgment; and he did not lose this because he remained pure in heart.[1]

1. cf. Job xxxiii, 9.

29

'Now it was a sabbath day when Jesus made the clay and opened his eyes. The Pharisees again asked him how he had received his sight. And he said to them, "He put clay on my eyes, and I washed, and I see." Some of the Pharisees said, "This man is not from God, for he does not keep the sabbath." '

John ix, 14–16

'This man is not from God...'

We must admit that we feel so confident, so sure of being men of God ourselves, that we can serenely and, as it were, casually, judge other men at the first glance with an expert eye, not only some men but almost all. 'You see so-and-so? He is not a man of God.' Sometimes we add, to ourselves or publicly, in a low voice or in stentorian ringing tones, 'You see so-and-so? You notice how hard he tries to look like a spiritually-minded man? Well—just the opposite—he is a real devil.' This is when we pronounce a considered and explicit judgment. But what about all the things we make up about our neighbours? It is very rarely that when we imagine things about him we imagine anything good. We are inclined—inclined on a precipitous slope! —to think ill of others. As soon as we see a man we concoct a whole romance about him, naturally a 'thriller'. Everything, even zeal, serves as a starting point to arrive at an unfavourable verdict.

101

I would be false to myself, to God and my readers, if I were to deny that in conducting these brief spiritual examinations, in making these spiritual soundings, I have to hold myself in check, as one would hold in a horse on a dangerous road. I swerve to the right and left, think of Tom, Dick or Harry, remember some moralist's famous adage, and am tempted to quote the witticism of a great dramatic poet, or linger over the memory of a scathing orator. I would like to be now witty, now elegiac, now melodramatic, now lyrical. Blinkers are not enough, a firm hand is needed on the reins, and sharp and cruel spurs. To concentrate on God and the soul requires a great effort, an inflexible purpose. The confession of such weakness does not spring from any desire to draw attention to myself—at least I hope not; it is intended rather to give an actual example, *in corpore vili* so to speak, of the fantastic and monstrous fertility of our evil thoughts, which immediately set about begetting and multiplying, and plotting together so that in a flash they can assert themselves with unheard of power. Then it is incredibly hard to dispossess them, drive them out and rid one's mind of them. They are like bacilli and microbes, capable of infecting the soul and destroying it with sin.

Our discontent with our wretched 'body of death', our distress when we discover its perpetual mutability, its vulnerability to disease and its dull resistance to the spirit, are felt also in the spiritual sphere. The sight of so much infirmity in good and obstinacy in evil, the noise and confusion of the unending conflict, the feeling of being powerless to resist and of being wounded even before we are struck, the intermingling of black darkness and pale glimmers of light, of abundant fear and scanty courage, and at times the suffering of all our most secret and intimate feelings, tears from our hearts the cry of St Paul: 'Who will free me from this body of death?'

The man who is truly fighting in the spiritual combat, the man in the thick of the battle, is not in a hurry to claim the victory; he does not say he has won, he does not lightly boast of being a man of God. The man who knows by experience how wretched and helpless he is can be no braggart. The braggart is found in the rear of the trenches. A trench in an advanced position teaches many things, above all moderation and modesty. How comes it then that we are so sure of being men of God that we can judge other men at first sight, and assert that they serve not God but the devil? Does this judgment itself not rather prove the contrary, that is, that we ourselves are not men of God? or at least that in this respect we are not his?

The Lord expounded one of his most illuminating and brilliant parables about the judgments we men are wont to deal out, right, left and centre: the parable of the Pharisee and the publican. And in the passage quoted above he shows us this sort of condemnation applied to himself: 'This man is not from God.' And even 'we know that this man is a sinner'. Just listen to it: 'we *know*'! They knew! And from what source did they draw this knowledge, if not from our customary source, the tainted source of pride?

30

'*Soon afterwards he went to a city called Nain, and his disciples and a great crowd went with him. As he drew near to the gate of the city, behold, a man who had died was being carried out, the only son of his mother, and she was a widow; and a large crowd from the city was with her. And when the Lord saw her, he had compassion on her and said to her, "Do not weep." And he came and touched the bier, and the bearers stood still. And he said, "Young man, I say to you, arise." And the dead man sat up, and began to speak. And he gave him to his mother.*'

Luke vii, 11–15

'He gave him to his mother'

Every time some misfortune befalls us we say: 'This is God's doing.' This is very human but also unjust. Instead, when things are going fairly well, we never even think of him. It looks almost as if the general impression is that God is one who takes things away from us. We can never be persuaded that all that we are and have constitutes a free gift from him, and that, in fact, it is exceptional for God to take anything away. He is generally the one who gives, and he gives everything. No one else can give—only God. In the same way, it is generally at the end of our life, not at the beginning, that our thoughts turn to him. We realize, if we realize anything at all, that we have to make our accounts with him; but we do not realize that in the beginning it was he who gave us those talents of which we have to render him an account.

In the parable of the talents the Lord described a certain kind of person who resembles us from this point of view: a man who was so obsessed with the thought of the accounts he had to render to his severely meticulous master that as a precaution he decided to bury the whole sum, so as to be able to return it to him just as it was, without profit, to be sure, but equally without loss. A foolish fellow, you will say, but we who always think of God as a merciless tax collector, always taking from us some possession, or someone dear to us, or something we delight in, one who will in the end take our very lives—are we not equally foolish?

This bereaved mother, seeing her son restored to her, could hardly believe her eyes. It couldn't be true. She looked at Jesus, and then at her son, and couldn't turn her gaze from him. There he was alive, and yet nobody ever comes back from death. Even we, reading that story after so many centuries, are moved to tears. It is without doubt one of the most poignant and delightful scenes of the New Testament. When Jesus meets a mother, he seems to feel for her respect, affection, almost veneration. It is as if he breathed the air of our Lady. No human creature came nearer to him than one mother, his own, our Lady. For her beauty and greatness he who was so chary of working miracles worked them all, the most beautiful and the most unbelievable. Without impairing her humility he made of her a miraculous creature, a star to outshine all others. No affectation, no sentimentality, no flattery—he gave her infinite suffering and infinite glory, with no diminishment or evasion, no way of escape.

.   .   .   .   .

Jesus, who had made, and continued to make, his mother so great, perhaps saw—indeed he foresaw everything—what his mother would suffer that evening when she was to see him die, and have him taken to the sepulchre and buried. While that other mother drew near to him he saw Mary, also a widow and still young, with her son too, dead in the flower of his youth. He saw this, and his heart was touched and he brought this other son back to life, and consoled his mother.

But do we need to think that in order to feel compassion for this mother Jesus had to think of his own? We men need this sort of prompting because, shut in our own minds, we measure all things by our own feelings. It is not so with Jesus. As God, he fully understands the feelings of every one of us, better and more profoundly than we understand ourselves; he knows us more intimately than we know ourselves. And as Man, who came in order to bear the sins of every one of us, he was not only that particular Man, but in a sense every man. His heart was, as it were, the heart of our own hearts. He understood and saw very clearly what that mother's heart was feeling. And he gave her back her son, without waiting for her to beg him to do so.

.   .   .   .   .

Let us think sometimes of our Father in Heaven above all for what he gives us. What have we that he has not given us? He has given us life, and the world; he has given us his Son and his Spirit; he has promised us himself. Even if he takes something away, what he gives is always greater than what he takes. Even pain is his gift. When he is severe with us it is really his way of being merciful. We must not strive with him, like fretful children, if sometimes he removes a loved object. And we must not be always asking for more. Let us rather thank him, and never stop thanking him. The world is so beautiful, our soul is so great, the coming of his Son such a mercy, the continual outpouring of his Spirit such a source of life and fire of love, his promises so unbelievably generous and yet so certain, that really we ought not to come before him always with sour looks, avoiding his glance, always with new recriminations in our hearts and foolish requests on our lips. Our accounts never come right and this is not through our fault (we seem to be saying) but because he has not given us enough—he, God, has not given us enough!

31

'Now Jesus loved Martha and her sister and Lazarus. So when he heard that he was ill, he stayed two days longer in the place where he was. Then after this he said to the disciples, "Let us go into Judea again." The disciples said to him, "Rabbi, the Jews were but now seeking to stone you, and are you going there again?" Jesus answered, "Are there not twelve hours in the day? If any one walks in the day he does not stumble, because he sees the light of this world. But if any one walks in the night, he stumbles, because the light is not in him." Thus he spoke, and then he said to them, "Our friend Lazarus has fallen asleep, but I go to awake him out of sleep ... let us go to him." Thomas, called the Twin, said to his fellow disciples, "Let us also go, that we may die with him." '

John xi, 5–16

'. . . are you going there again?'

Their anxiety was very reasonable. They knew that if he went back among his enemies he would die in their hands, or at least run the risk of being killed: why then did he wish to return among them? why not avoid them? But Jesus was not concerned about this. At other times he had avoided this sort of encounter. One day in his own village they had tried to hurl him over a precipice. Another time, elsewhere, they had been about to stone him, but he had miraculously slipped out of their hands. This time, no. This time he had no need to be warned and set on his guard, for on several occasions he had already announced the manner of his death. His was not a presentiment or merely the remembrance of a prophecy; it was divine foreknowledge. He foresaw all. And he went back, into the midst of the conspirators, where the poisonous adders lay in ambush. He went back without the slightest hesitation or uncertainty.

.　　　.　　　.　　　.　　　.

O Jesus, what a lesson for us! In moments such as this we always gather around you, begging and imploring you, with good advice and the best intentions, to protect your honour and your life, in your mystical body if no longer in your own person. You listen to what we say, look us in the eyes, and go your own road. Yes, your road, that dreaded road of yours, may one day be ours; we ought not to hesitate a moment, but follow you at once. It is the Way of the Cross. Either we follow you along that way, or we forsake you for ever.

It may not always be, but it might easily be (as it has been for so many of our brothers in the faith) the road to death and martyrdom; it will certainly mean doing our duty to the end, possibly under fire. The most insignificant duty, just because it is a duty, that is the will of God, can sometimes jeopardize our lives. What could there be more cheerful than the celebration of a wedding? Suddenly two hired cut-throats appear in the road, and poor Don Abbondio is within a hair's breadth of martyrdom.[1] Do not let us deceive ourselves— the musket shots that scared the life out of Don Abbondio may be heard by us all at any street corner, any bend in the road, or even on our own doorstep. There is no duty that does not sooner or later cost us a peck of trouble; sometimes

---

1. An allusion to the famous incident in chapter 1 of Manzoni's novel *The Betrothed*, the timid priest Don Abbondio's encounter with the local tyrant's hired ruffians.

anguish of heart, less often but often enough a real and considerable sacrifice. Or life itself? Yes, even life itself.

·   ·   ·   ·   ·

If by this time I have any readers left, one of them may
say: I do not find that doing one's duty is such a tragic business. You, Sir Writer, exaggerate. Tell me the truth—are
you not a bit of a Jansenist? My answer to this hypothetical
reader is that I am no Jansenist: my favourite author is St
Alphonsus de' Liguori. I mention this, not to talk about myself, but to avoid any shade of misunderstanding between us.
I am no Jansenist—but, to tell the truth, I find it very hard
to be good and, as you see, I must confess that I do not even
succeed. You instead, Sir Reader, succeed and apparently
with ease. But are you quite sure you succeed? Do you make
a brief examination of conscience every evening? You will not
deny that the saints (real saints, complete with altars, haloes,
miracles, devoted followers and all the rest) did not share
your supreme self-confidence. To hear them speak one would
have taken them for the worst of sinners, they did nothing
right, they never found the just measure in anything; either
they sinned by excess or by default; some of them insisted on
going to confession every day. And you, my good Reader, tell
the truth—after all no one overhears us here—you go to
confession at Easter, if at all. Your conscience does not worry
you—in fact it is a source of pride for you. You place your
hand on your heart and say: 'My conscience. . . .' Nor does
your soul give you the slightest trouble. Perhaps it is asleep
most of the time. Perhaps, but God forbid! it may even suffer
from sleeping sickness. Who knows—it may be already dead,
and you speak of it as if it were still alive. 'He went on fighting, and he was already dead.'[1]

There is a rule that admits of no exceptions: the more we
try to do good, the more we feel that the good done is nothing
compared with what still remains to be done. The more
watchful we are, the more we see how many things still es-

1. F. Berni: *Orlando Innamorato*, canto 53, octave 60.

cape our notice. The further we proceed, at a good pace, along God's road, the more it stretches endlessly away before us. To live like Christians is a heroic thing, and heroism is not made up of a few fine words and gestures. There is no commandment—let alone the Counsels of Perfection—which at some time or other does not impose very grave sacrifices. If at the first hint of sacrifices we start to retreat, and sacrifice our souls for the sake of our comfort, then we are but counterfeit Christians.

The world would not have slipped back into paganism almost everywhere, as it has done, if we had been Christians in fact as well as in name. We loudly ask why there is so much apostasy; and we find vigorous answers and convenient solutions. It would be enough for Christians to be really Christians, and all other people would follow suit. Why is it that we are not really Christian? The answer is quite clear: true Christians often have to choose that dreaded road which his disciples tried to deter Jesus from taking—when he would not listen to them and resolutely set out upon it. That road, like all other self-respecting roads, has a name: *Via Crucis*, the Way of the Cross.

32

'Again Jesus spoke to them, saying, "I am the light of the world; he who follows me will not walk in darkness, but will have the light of life." The Pharisees then said to him, "You are bearing witness to yourself; your testimony is not true." Jesus answered, "Even if I do bear witness to myself, my testimony is true, for I know whence I have come and whither I am going. You judge according to the flesh, I judge no one. Yet even if I do judge, my judgment is true, for it is not I alone that judge, but I and he who sent me." '

John viii, 12–16

'I judge no one'

And we judge everyone. Not a soul escapes our merciless fire. To see, judge and condemn is the work of a moment, like Caesar's *'veni, vidi, vici'*. One glance, and the bird is down. Among the greatest qualities and gifts, with which we are so generously endowed, are our clear-sightedness, and rapid, accurate judgment. Our Lord, judge of the living and the dead, took pleasure in an attribute that was precisely and diametrically the opposite: 'I judge no one.' This is not the only difference between Jesus and ourselves, but it is considerable.

Jesus had all the qualifications for passing judgment: authority, knowledge, conscience. And he judged no one. He came on earth to save, not to condemn. We have none of the necessary qualifications, and yet we never stop judging our neighbour. Jesus, even when he instituted the sacrament of penitence, wanted the guilty party, and no one else, to be the accuser, while the judge who is in the place of Jesus, that is the confessor, can accept only the accusation which the guilty party himself proffers. We judge in the absence of the accused, and without knowing anything about him. This is unforgivable, but it is even worse than that: it is not our duty to judge. On the contrary, we are forbidden to do so. It is therefore a criminal act on our part to arrogate to ourselves this function—it is rank disobedience. We have no real knowledge of the facts, and our conscience is not adequately trained and informed for this task. Nevertheless, we take a delight in passing judgment, cheerfully and with a festive air, and with pride: it is always a pleasure.

We ourselves are debtors of divine justice, we are contumacious and fugitives, afraid at every moment of being collared by the law. But meanwhile we lay hold of our brothers and condemn them with unpardonable ferocity. Our Lord once described us in stinging words, in his parable of the debtor whose debts were cancelled by his master and who, when given time to settle his accounts with his own debtor, seized him by the throat and clapped him into gaol. A thought to make the hair on our heads rise on end—if we have heads for our hair to rise on!

And it must not be thought that this matter of not judging our fellows is a mere unimportant detail in Christian behaviour—a bit of superfluous decoration, a purely academic question of form. Jesus has put the whole of this commandment in the Our Father, and made its meaning and implications very clear. He has slipped it all in (if we may use such an expression about the Lord) so that either we have to swallow it whole, to our advantage, or let it stick in our throat and choke us. Forgive us as we forgive others. It is like saying: be as kind to us as we are kind to our fellow men. It would be a poor prospect for us if God were to treat us as we treat our fellows. Yet, this is how it will be. Nevertheless we go cheerfully on our way, distributing to right and left our bold, speedy, careless judgments and condemnations.

It is no use deciding, in theory, not to pronounce any more judgments. The harm lies not so much in pronouncing them as in forming them. If a man who always judged his neighbour harshly were to confine his virtuous intention merely to keeping his opinions to himself, in the end he would either burst or go mad. One cannot cultivate and water a plant and then insist that it neither grow nor yield flowers and fruit. We must educate ourselves interiorly not to judge others harshly, in fact, not to judge them at all.

But how is it possible, you will say, to refrain from passing judgment? If you have two eyes in your head and you meet a cripple or a hunchback you cannot help seeing them, you cannot help noticing their physical defects. Seeing is in itself a sort of judgment. The same is true of moral defects. There you are, minding your own business, and someone turns up who is evil-tongued, insolent, vain, an idiot or a knave, an expert twister—how is it possible not to see what he is? One cannot stand there inert, without forming some sort of opinion.

This is what you must do. Let us say you meet a hunchback, but if your own hump is bigger than his you will certainly not feel tempted to point out that innocent and unfortunate man's deformity, with a coarse and cruel jest. The pity of it is that you, a hunchback, do not see your own hump. But if you could but see it, and see how ugly it is, you wouldn't stare so hard at other people's shoulders. Remember we were not born to judge. We were born to be judged, and God have pity on us!

33

*'The Jews answered him, "Are we not right in saying that
you are a Samaritan and have a demon?" Jesus answered,
"I have not a demon; but I honour my Father and you dishonour me. Yet I do not seek my own glory; there is One
who seeks it and he will be the judge. Truly, truly, I say to
you, if anyone keeps my word, he will never see death." '*

John viii, 48–51

'... he will never see death'

It may seem a paradox, but no days were so triumphant as
those days of the Passion. Not only in their memory and
celebration, but also in the events themselves, the obscure and
painful sufferings of Jesus, there breathes such a tenderness,
and such sublimity, that the story is both a lament and a
hymn of praise. It is indeed the final challenge, the last duel
between life and death; and we already know who will be the
victor, in spite of the insults, outrage, ignominy, countless
wounds, the blood and the bleeding to death. The battle has
been joined, before the astonished heavens and, alas! the in-
difference of men. Except for the terror-stricken apostles and
those poor heroic women, the people do not understand what
is about to take place. One day they will understand, and the
bare account of the Passion will become for them the tale
most frequently told and yet most unutterable. No tragedy

114

will be more often re-enacted, no battle more famous in song, no love more profoundly shared. Greek tragedy was not so beautiful; no epic of adventure or warfare, of love or death, will ever surpass the four accounts given by the four Evangelists. The grandest music, most worthy of God and most loved of men, has been inspired by their words. The greatest art has despaired of being able to carve or paint or describe those faces, those deeds, those moments and hours.

The Passion begins, with its pain and terror; and yet the sky is lit with flights of angels, the chanting of hymns, gleams of glory. The Passion begins, and never before has the voice of Jesus sounded so firm and authoritative, or so deeply pierced our hearts and, if one may say so, the heart of God. Never has Jesus spoken so much about life, with such energy, strength and gentleness. The days became darker and crueller, the people around him more bitter and full of menace; the plot was thickening and yet, as if by some divine translucency, the nearer the man in Jesus drew to his ordeal of pain, the more brightly God shone through the man Jesus. Never was he more truly life itself than on the eve and in the hour of his death. Everything in him attained its peak, its climax. When he spoke of love it was inconceivably infinite and profound. When he spoke of our union with God no union could have seemed more real, and yet more improbable and miraculous—'that they may be one even as we are one', he prayed.[1] When he spoke of leaving some remembrance of himself, that remembrance was the Eucharist. When he took leave of his disciples their last meal together was the Last Supper, and his words of farewell the will and testament of a God who had become man for love of men, and was about to be killed by men. He accepted death at their hands and by so doing brought them salvation. When he spoke of men he used the tenderest terms: they were the branches, he was the vine; they were his friends, brothers, sons, children, they were part of himself. When he spoke of the Father, and the treasures of the Father's life, it was to assure us that they are all ours. As if it were not enough for men to have

1. John xvii, 22.

received the Son he promised that when the Son went away the Holy Spirit would descend like fire.

It is a strange thing, but all the rest of the Gospel seems no more than the prologue to the Passion. The Passion contains the whole story of Jesus, the story of all men, of every man. It is the principal occurrence, the main action, the event which in a certain sense means more than the creation, because it is a second creation, and is followed not by sin, like the former creation, but by the forgiveness of sin and the restoration of all things—indeed, a restoration of more than was ever lost.

The mere thought of the Passion makes us love our Father and brothers with a love which springs from the Heart of Christ and which he left to us so that it might be the only valid sign by which we could recognize each other and know our own hearts also. We can no longer banish Jesus from our thoughts—we would like to run through the streets stopping everyone and saying to them: Jesus is dying. He is dying for you. And you? Where are you going? What are you doing? What are we all doing? He is dying for us, and we do not even think of him.

No days are so melancholy and yet so full of joy, so dark with death and radiant with life, now like a funeral, now like a wedding. The winter is over: rise, my soul; the spring is here and will last for ever; life is here, to die no more. This is the radiance of eternity. We mourn over the death of Jesus but before our mourning chants have died away we hear the first loud imperious trumpet peals hailing the resurrection. Jesus has died, Jesus lives for ever. Our sins are washed away, our death yields to life eternal.

34

'On the last day of the feast, the great day, Jesus stood up and proclaimed, "If anyone thirst, let him come to me and drink. He who believes in me, as the Scripture has said, 'Out of his heart shall flow rivers of living water.'" Now this he said about the Spirit, which those who believed in him were to receive, for as yet the Spirit had not been given, because Jesus was not yet glorified.'

John vii, 37–9

'If anyone thirst . . .'

If we thirst . . .? But our thirst, Lord, is never slaked. We stoop to drink from every spring, and there and then we feel satisfied, but a few moments later our thirst returns. We die of thirst, O Lord. You say that if we come to you to drink our thirst will be slaked for ever. We find it hard to believe what you say.

We have tried, and we still try, every source. We have appealed to everyone, we have been everywhere, to assuage our thirst. We thought philosophy would content us, but we were swollen without being satisfied. We turned to the arts, but for all their beauty they could do nothing for us; they inebriated us like sweet wine, but we were still thirsty. We had recourse to learning, and with the brains you gave us, Lord, we have as day followed day possessed ourselves of one secret

117

after another of the vast machinery of this world. We have invented the electric lamp and the aeroplane, but also the direst weapons of slaughter, and the atomic bomb. We fling ourselves into action, but activity wearies us and gives us no peace. As for pleasure, the less said the better; in the mad rush for pleasure we destroy ourselves and become beasts. 'If anyone thirst . . .' you say. We are thirsting all our days, Lord. We have become a longing, a cry, a prayer. Nothing contents us, everything tempts and incites us.

It is because we were made for you, and you alone. The world is essentially a reflection of you and as we pursue these reflected lights each fills us with enthusiasm for a brief moment, and then we once more resume the mad chase after what dazzles but does not illuminate, seizes us but cannot hold us, pleases but cannot content, promises but fails to keep its promise. Your voice tells us to follow the streams up to their source, to follow the reflected rays to the fire that sends them forth, to rise from the effects to the cause. We hear your voice but we do not heed it. A cursed restlessness, like the incurable delirium of a fever, agitates us and holds us back from seeking you. It breaks us to pieces, scattering us upon things that pass away. We do not succeed in being 'all of a piece' in ourselves. And the reason for this is certainly because we shall never find our own integrity until we are reconciled to your will. We want to straighten ourselves out, and we get more and more entangled. We try to simplify ourselves according to our own will, not yours. The strongest among us do indeed succeed in becoming more purposeful, but only by placing themselves blindly at the service of a great passion. They yield control over themselves to a master, sometimes avarice, or vanity, or ambition, and so they become enormously rich and powerful and famous. But with all this, what have they succeeded in doing? Death comes to break the spell, and devouring thirst reappears, and they too die of thirst, with burning hearts and parched lips, without a blade of grass springing from a good deed, or the relief and refreshment of a drop of the water that flows to eternal life. They die, and fall into another and crueller fire, they burn of thirst among the eternal flames, and their thirst too will endure for ever.

It is thirst for you, O Lord. No words of yours are more merciful than those you say to us today. Whoever thirsts for God, you say, must come to Me and drink. Your first faithful followers heard this and understood, and they depicted you in the image of a fountain, at which sheep were drinking their fill, or sometimes, in the great mosaics, they put this fountain under your feet, and showed rivers flowing out of it, to water the world that was parched by the fires lit by the Enemy, and by the fevers of our lusts. The man who thirsts for God, and does not drink from your pure well, will die of thirst; and every man thirsts for God. This is our history, the story of our soul. Whoever has even once found your spring flowing above his road will never drink from any other source; and if he rejects you he will die of thirst.

We pray to you, O Lord, we who kneel on the verge of your divine stream, and adroitly or clumsily, and at times with a great effort, moisten our lips and find refreshment, and we pray for all who have forsaken you, the fountain of living water, and have built for themselves cisterns, 'broken cisterns that cannot hold the water'.[1] We pray also for all those— and because of our own inertia there are still so many—who have not yet found you, the only Oasis in the desert of this world.

We are all thirsty, and you, you alone, are water for our thirst.

1. Jeremiah ii, 13.

35

'Now the Jews' feast of Tabernacles was at hand. So his brethren said to him, "Leave here and go to Judea, that your disciples may see the works you are doing. For no man works in secret if he seeks to be known openly. If you do these things, show yourself to the world." For even his brethren did not believe in him. Jesus said to them: "My time has not yet come, but your time is always here. The world cannot hate you, but it hates me because I testify of it that its works are evil."'

John vii, 2–7

'Even his brethren did not believe in him'

Who these 'brethren' were is no longer a problem for anyone, although fifty years ago the most ferocious battles, between believers and unbelievers, were fought over them. Certainly they were not brothers as we understand the term today. They were relatives, perhaps even close relatives.

St John clearly states, in the above passage, that although they were closely related to Jesus they were very far from him spiritually; they did not believe in him. Elsewhere another Evangelist is even more explicit: they thought that Jesus was a fanatic or madman or, in the kindest of hypotheses, a fool.

The family is no chance combination of circumstances; it

is of divine origin. In the New Covenant, moreover, Jesus raised matrimony to the state of a Sacrament. We must therefore never dream of putting the blame on the family, matrimony, or blood relationship, and of seeing these, as many do today, as the root of all evils. Unhappily, men make incredible accusations and denials when their hearts are ruled by passion; and, as is the case with every other institution, family ties become burdensome when the rules of family life are broken, or about to be broken. Today the family is being attacked on all sides, and the Catholic Church is alone in defending her essence and her integrity.

Nevertheless, we must bear in mind that the family itself, unless it lives a shared Christian life, in substance as in form, may constitute a serious obstacle to the spiritual life, and cause considerable trouble, even frustrating it and making it impossible. When father and mother, parents and children all think in terms of material interests, they form together a sort of society with an accumulated strength, so that their materialism acquires a power which it is difficult to resist. Most painful situations may arise from this; if a selfish father uses his paternal dignity and authority to prop up and further his own selfishness, it may happen that a son, who may not be selfish himself, may anger and disobey his father. If a mother is vain and ambitious, and if her daughter, by some strange chance, is neither vain nor ambitious, innumerable conflicts may arise, most painful and embarrassing. All the members of a family may be at odds with each other. Irremovable barriers are set up between people bound by the closest ties. Tragedies occur, in which a man's worst enemies are the people he loves most.

Not even our Lord himself escaped this poignant grief: his own kith and kin conspired with his most determined enemies—those who were to put him to death. We must remember that the family too, if it wishes to fulfil its natural destiny as a family, and be worthy of the supernatural graces it receives, must live a Christian family life. Instead, this institution also has been affected by the conviction prevalent in all State organizations: that is, that its members need not hold any idea or faith in common and every one of them should live a life apart.

This may seem like a victory for freedom, but just think what a tragedy would ensue if each of the various organs of the body were to set up a liberal independent government, if our head said it wished to be free to lead its own life, if our stomach had the same idea, and our liver, lungs, blood and nerves expressed the same desire—and if all were, in the name of liberty, to refuse to share the same common life!

36

'The Jews took up stones again to stone him. Jesus answered them, "I have shown you many good works from the Father, for which of these do you stone me?" The Jews answered him, "We stone you for no good work but for blasphemy; because you, being a man, make yourself God." Jesus answered them, "Is it not written in your law 'I said, you are Gods'? If he called them Gods to whom the word of God came (and scripture cannot be broken) do you say of him whom the Father consecrated and sent into the world, 'You are blaspheming', because I said I am the Son of God?"'

John x, 31–6

'...for which of these good works do you stone me?'

Jesus seems to say to us: I have created Heaven and earth for you, and the whole universe. I have created life. In the order of living things I have set man in the topmost place. I have created you, a man among men.

I have not caused you to be born in barbarian times or in savage lands. I have given you life in the fulness of time, in the heart of the civilized world, amid a wealth of arts and sciences. Your own city may be one of the most famous in history, your own village may be one of the most beautiful. But even if it were a hamlet on a hilltop or at the bottom of a valley, or a few houses lost in an endless plain, you cannot deny its charm, or the fact that to you it is the dearest corner of the world.

You can say without exaggeration: 'my own town', or 'my own village'. You are right, it is yours and you belong to it.

I caused you to be born in your own particular family, whether it be rich or poor, fortunate or wretched, half dead or full of life, its members sickly or in good health. This also belongs to you, as a nest to a bird. It belongs to you and to your brothers and sisters. The family is intended for the birth and upbringing of children. Perhaps your family does not love you—could this be your own fault? If it is not your fault you feel it is a great misfortune, and you long for the affection of your own folk.

In calling you into life, I have endowed you with certain qualities, of strength or health, genius or skill. If you think you have received nothing from me, it is evidently the greedy desire to possess even more that makes you think this. Concentrate your thoughts on what you have, not on what you lack. Without a doubt you have something, even if not all you desire. There is no man alive without a rich and varied endowment of humanity. Merely to be a man is not a gift to be lightly esteemed or measured.

I have kept beside you every day of your life. Although you have been unaware of me, as you have been unaware of the beauty of the world extending within and around you, I have always been close at hand. This is not a bright idea of theologians—it is an actual fact that your life is a continuing creation of mine. You would sink back into nothingness, with the rest of the created world, if my providence did not at every moment uphold what I have created. Today even the physicists tell you this, that the world is the continuing and wonderful creation of a loving intelligence. Just fancy: even the physicists . . .!

When I created you at the beginning of time I was not content merely to make you a man, I raised you to the wondrous dignity of an adopted Son of God. In the person of your absolute Master I have given you a Father. I have given you the right to call him Father, and to consider yourself, for all temporal and eternal purposes, his son, a sharer in his life and an heir to his glory.

I have redeemed you. I could have redeemed you with an act of my will. Instead, I came down to tread your roads. I put on your mortal flesh. I took on my shoulders all your responsibilities before God, all your relations with your brothers, all your suffering and distress.

I have loved you with a love that has, and can have, no equal, a love so great that it will always be beyond your understanding. I have refused you no greatness and no joy. My promises are more firm than the heavens themselves. Heaven and earth will pass away, but my words will not pass away.[1]

I have always granted your prayers, except when you have asked me for things which you should have been ashamed to ask for, or things which you did not realize would hurt you. For you I opened wide my arms upon the Cross, and my arms are still open to you, waiting for you.

For which of these works do you hate me, flee from me, assault and crucify me?

1. Matthew xxiv, 35.

37

'One of the Pharisees asked him to eat with him, and he went into the Pharisee's house, and sat at table. And behold, a woman of the city, who was a sinner, when she learned that he was sitting at table in the Pharisee's house, brought an alabaster flask of ointment, and standing behind him at his feet, weeping, she began to wet his feet with her tears, and wiped them with the hair of her head, and kissed his feet, and anointed them with the ointment. Now when the Pharisee who had invited him saw it, he said to himself, "If this man were a prophet, he would have known who and what sort of woman this is who is touching him, for she is a sinner." ... Turning toward the woman Jesus said to Simon, "Do you see this woman? I entered your house, you gave me no water for my feet, but she has wet my feet with her tears and wiped them with her hair. You gave me no kiss, but from the time I came in she has not ceased to kiss my feet. You did not anoint my head with oil, but she has anointed my feet with ointment. Therefore I tell you, her sins, which are many, are forgiven. ..."'

Luke vii, 36–47

'I entered your house'

Simon the Pharisee cannot have been a bad man. The Lord accepted his invitation and sat down at his table. But then just see what happened! Into the house of this man, a Pharisee and a good fellow, came a woman, and a woman with the worst possible reputation. She came to look for Jesus and, finding him there reclining at the table, she began to show him such marks of affection and tenderness that all who were present were horrified. Some blushed for shame, the host was on thorns, his face full of dismay and embarrassment. And, to be just, if this sort of thing had happened in our own home we should have been beside ourselves with rage and indignation. Such an intolerable situation!

The Pharisee boiled with anger, but did not know what to do. He had nothing against Jesus; in fact until now he had rather liked him, but now he was beginning to hate him. The whole thing was past a joke. There were respectable women present, and friends of his in high office, there were—the good Pharisee must have said—there were children present. What did all this demonstration of affection mean? And he—didn't he know who that woman was? If not, what sort of prophet was he?

When the Lord enters into the house of our soul we can never be sure that he will fit in with our notions of etiquette and good manners. He compared himself to fire,[1] and said that his was not a carefully guarded domestic fire but one which was to spread and burn and destroy everything it touched. Our wretched precautions and miserable hypocrisy are of no avail when Jesus enters our house. It is better to keep him out; but if we once let him in, everything we keep most prudently hidden comes out at once into the open; and everything we like to exhibit, pinned carefully to our walls, is blown away on the wind.

.   .   .   .   .

Our respectability, our distinction (not a very Christian term, anyway), our position and standard of living seem to be things for which the Lord has little regard. I may be the most respectable of men, but he allows me to die of the same illness as that which strikes down the meanest of human creatures.

1. cf. Luke xii, 49.

He saves Lazarus, sitting amid the dogs and the litter of the streets, and condemns the rich man with his purple and fine linen. He sits at the table with the Pharisee and not only compares him with that unhappy woman but says outright, in the presence of all, that the Pharisee suffers by this comparison, because she is worth more than he. Turning to that woman, guilty of the most shameful loves, he speaks of love, of the love of God; he accepts her love and answers it with his own, the love of a God. And if that woman was, as many surmise, Mary Magdalen, how lovingly was Jesus to reward that heroic act of repentance!

.   .   .   .   .

Truly Jesus does not respect our code or conform to our standards; he does not obey those rules which we respect more highly than the law of God itself. Not that we should presume on the supreme naturalness and radiant simplicity of Jesus—but we might at least try to be just a little less hypocritical and pay a little more attention to our conscience. We might be a little less attached to appearances. In God's sight how shall we appear? We shall appear as we are. . . .

38

'Many of the Jews, therefore, who had come with Mary and had seen what he did, believed on him; but some of them went to the Pharisees and told them what Jesus had done. . . . One of them, Caiaphas, who was high priest that year, said to them, "You know nothing at all; you do not understand that it is expedient for you that one man should die for the people, and that the whole nation should not perish." . . . So from that day on they took counsel how to put him to death. Jesus therefore no longer went about openly among the Jews, but went from there to the country near the wilderness, to a town called Ephraim; and there he stayed with the disciples.'

John xi, 45–54

'. . . he stayed with the disciples'

Jesus is not the sort of teacher who, at the end of his lesson, leaves his pupils to their own devices and goes about his own business. He is essentially our teacher; he does not make a profession of it, as we do, who are teachers at certain hours of the day, according to the time-table. He does not set himself up as a teacher, he *is* a teacher. He is our teacher, as truly as he is a man. It was for this purpose, among others, that he became man, in order to instruct us. So we must not be surprised when we find him staying with his disciples.

Moreover, and in this he differs from our proud human teachers, it is from his own life and behaviour that we learn from him. Even before he speaks he has taught us by his deeds. He 'began to do and teach'.[1] His very personality is a loving lesson. Merely by being near him we not only learn in theory but we receive the strength to put our learning to the test.

So the fact that Jesus stayed with his disciples and apostles does not surprise us, given the nature of the teacher and his work. Nor must we doubt that now he is in fact among us, in the midst of us, within us. What we doubt is something else; it is that, in spite of his closeness to us, we may be far from him. One can be in the sunlight and yet be too blind to see; one can be in a warm place and shiver with ague, or in the cold and burn with fever. One can live in the bosom of one's family, and be spiritually remote.

We have neighbours whom we meet several times a day, whose names are unknown to us and who are still strangers. We can say our prayers many times a day and constantly repeat: 'Lord, Lord!', and alas! know nothing about him and be such strangers to him as to be denied admittance to the courts of Heaven.

We do not doubt the constant presence of the Teacher among us; we doubt our own presence with him. In a furtive but determined way we try to withdraw from his presence. He is here, and we live as if he were absent; indeed, as if he did not even exist. We eliminate him from our thoughts, our affections, our occupations and anxieties. We make a place for him among the most useless and tiresome formalities required of us. What good does it do us, we think, to go to Mass on Sundays? And which of our prayers is ever granted? Thinking and speaking in this way we even have the brazen insolence to reproach him. But how attentive are we at Mass? Do we even know what the Mass is? And when do we listen to a sermon with the attention we give, let us say, to reading a newspaper? And when is any prayer of ours a living thing, aflame with faith and love? When is the presence of Jesus, in his adorable majesty and infinite goodness, felt as a real presence with us? He is greater and more beautiful than light

1. Acts i, 1.

itself, and yet we do not see him. Let us at least say with the blind man in the Gospel story: 'Lord, let me receive my sight.'[1] It is not enough, Lord, for you to be with me; you must open my eyes so that I may see you.

---

1. Luke xviii, 41.

39

'And Jesus answered them, "The hour has come for the Son of Man to be glorified. Truly, truly, I say to you, unless a grain of wheat falls into the earth and dies, it remains alone; but if it dies, it bears much fruit. He who loves his life loses it, and he who hates his life in this world will keep it for eternal life."'

John xii, 23–5

'... it remains alone'

Until we understand that we must sacrifice ourselves, if need be even to death, we shall remain alone, in the most hopeless solitude: without anyone, without God, without even ourselves. If the seed under the ground does not die it will not produce the ear of corn, and then what could it do? What use would it be? would its life be worth living? what sort of existence could it have? If it does not give birth to the ear of corn, if it does not function as a seed, it is nothing, or at least nothing of any value.

The parable (if we may so call it, and it deserves this name although it is not a narrative, merely an allusion), the parable of the seed is the parable of Jesus, and of ourselves. Jesus went on to the end. He was not content with fine ideas and good intentions. He truly died to himself, so to speak, in what he came to do. He gave away all that was divine in him, and all that was human. He spent himself entirely. He did not cling

132

on to one jot of honour, one moment of peace, one drop of blood. He died. That is why he is nearest to the Father in Heaven and his brothers are innumerable: he did not remain alone.

Now let us look at what we are and what we do. Our destiny is no different (except in its proportions, naturally) from the destiny of Jesus. He became a man like ourselves in order that we should at last understand, simply by looking at him, what man is and what is his life. Not that it is our job to redeem the world, but certainly not one of us will be redeemed unless he co-operates in his own salvation; and no man can co-operate in his own salvation unless he consents to co-operate, in so far as he can, in the salvation of others. Charity consists, substantially, in nothing else but this collaboration.

We shall not enter Heaven alone. No one who remains alone can enter Heaven. The love of God and the love of our neighbour exclude any possible solitude. Even in the world of men it is difficult to be alone. We are ringed round with matter, chained to the generations, bound to society; we were not made to be alone. In the supernatural order it is even less possible to be alone. Solitude is Hell, if Hell is hatred of God and hatred of our neighbour; hatred and therefore aversion. But even in hell we shall not be alone; we shall have the devils and the damned for company. Hell is, one might say, a multitude of solitary people: the ideal place for all who have wished to remain alone.

The Lord has plainly told us that there is only one way of escape from our solitude: self-sacrifice.

40

Matthew xxvi, 1–75; xxvii, 1–66

'The Passion of our Lord Jesus Christ. . . .'

No theme of poetry or music, no theme of love or remembrance, surpasses in sweetness or intensity those few words which herald the Gospel story of the Passion: 'The Passion of our Lord Jesus Christ.' Even when we say them our hearts are touched and our eyes soften with tears. No strains of distant music, when we are alone or ill, no sign of life, of returning life, when we have felt near to death, no word of loyalty and love when we are insulted and mocked and abandoned—nothing of all that touches our hearts most poignantly can be compared with these simple words. I remember a friend (he died years ago) who on Good Friday used to wander about the streets like a gentle maniac, and no one could say a word to him, because he was so full of the memory of Christ, so silent and so absorbed. Certainly he would never have spoken of Christ, as he never spoke of his immeasurable love for him; but one could see this love in his eyes, his face, his whole person. It is a terrible thing to have to speak, to have to write! And what if the best of ourselves were in our words, words which are at best but a cold exercise of the imagination, an essay composed for the occasion, a set speech! If there were nothing behind these words, what a tragedy!

St Thomas More was the greatest lawyer in London, a very

fine writer and a cultured Humanist scholar; he was Chancellor of England, had a very large family, and countless friends. Nevertheless, every Friday he spent the whole day apart, alone, thinking of the Passion of Jesus.

A priest (he too is dead, to our great loss) asked me, one day we spent together, if he had time to go into church for a moment. I had business to do that took me more than two hours; when I had finished I looked for him, remembered that he was in church, and felt ashamed I had left him there so long (I repeat: I was ashamed to have left him there, as if it were any ordinary place!), and ran into the church; he was kneeling there, looking very happy and with a peaceful radiance in his eyes. He was reading. I asked his pardon, and he begged me not to distress myself. I asked: 'But is the book you are reading so enthralling?' He answered: 'The book is certainly far from dull; but it is the subject matter which is so beautiful.' And he smiled at me with a gleam of tenderness and holy mischief in his eyes. It was the *Reflections on the Passion* of St. Alphonsus de' Liguori, who was so much in love with Jesus that he went into prolonged ecstasies every time he thought about the Passion.

We should know by heart the four Gospel accounts of the Passion—they would keep us wonderful company. There have been saints who knew all the Gospels, if not all the Bible, by heart; once even the least learned among the faithful learnt by heart, simply by attending church, immensely long passages of Holy Scripture, of the Fathers, and of writers of books of devotion. The details of the life of Jesus were better known than the details of our own familiar everyday life. And the Passion was the theme of themes. It was not enough to hear it in church in the liturgy of Holy Week; it was not enough to have it narrated over and over again by the preachers; it was represented in crude but powerful pageants in the middle of a town or village, while processions moved along every road, amidst a hundred lights and hymns. The Passion of Jesus, with the Crucified and our Lady of Sorrows, were the great devotions of the Christian people.

And what do we do about it today? What does the Passion

of Jesus mean for us? Does it mean nothing any more? Does it no longer surprise and enthral us? There will come a day—it must come—when our own sufferings will begin, and will end with our death. On that day the Church asks her ministers, after having pronounced the 'Go forth, Christian soul', to read to us the Passion of our Lord. We shall indeed be blessed if those words are familiar to our ears in that hour.

41

'Six days before the Passion, Jesus came to Bethany, where Lazarus was, whom Jesus had raised from the dead. There they made him a supper; Martha served, and Lazarus was one of those at table with him. Mary took a pound of costly ointment of pure nard and anointed the feet of Jesus and wiped his feet with her hair; and the house was filled with the fragrance of the ointment.'

John xii, 1–3

'the house was filled with the fragrance of the ointment'

A good deed fills the house with a sweet odour. We speak of the odour of sanctity, and the expression is apt. When we notice this odour we feel at once what Dante, who was generally pointed and precise in his descriptions, could only call 'something unknown, indistinct'. A single flower is company in a house, more for its perfume than for its beauty. Its perfume seems homely to us, and not only pleases but consoles.

Good deeds have a sweet odour which they exhale and spread all around, to rejoice our souls. They are the best kind of charity we can show to our neighbour, and are always refreshingly new, as if seen for the first time. In this respect too they resemble a sweet odour because, when this is really sweet, it is like a new discovery. On the contrary, a bad smell makes us cry out with disgust: 'What a pestilential stench! Where have I noticed that before?' What is not good but bad,

137

and bad for us, has a staleness about it, perhaps because we are so experienced in suffering that we seem to recognize every kind of discomfort: it is as if we had known all pain and very little pleasure. This is also because pain is more persistent than joy. We never miss any particle of suffering whereas, when joy comes, we never manage to relish it to the full.

The pleasant custom of occasionally offering our friends the affectionate token of a bunch of flowers is very charming, and would give even more pleasure if it did not frequently become merely a gallant gesture or a formal convention. Why do we not offer, instead of flowers, a bunch of good deeds? Only schoolgirls and novices still observe this custom of offering a sort of 'spiritual bouquet', generally composed of tiny acts of mortification, secretly offered to God, and counted like the Hail Marys of a rosary. If we bothered to find out the origin of this pious practice, and if we did not always make our bouquet consist of mortifications, the custom might become popular again with all Christians. It would offer refreshment to some parched and embittered hearts. It is true that a good deed nearly always costs a sacrifice, but we should be sour and surly folk indeed if we always laid more stress on the sacrifice a good deed requires than on the good it does to others. Even if we give flowers we have to pay for them, but if the man who presented a bouquet were visibly concerned at the thought of how much it had cost him, he would do better not to buy it, and not to offer it. Unhappily, we usually behave in this way with God, and with men,—we present the bill. Our face expresses anxiety, our heart clamours to be repaid, and at once. We place a candle on the altar, and become impatient if our prayer is not immediately granted.

.   .   .   .   .

The air of our houses, our factories and offices, our cities and now even our countryside, is poisoned, not so much by the fumes of petrol and all the other aids to our comfort, to which we have become enslaved, as by the stench of our wickedness. Let us refresh with the perfume of a good deed an atmosphere so heavy with poisons. Among so many bad smells let us insert a fragrance. Let us weave into the thick webs of treachery a smile of true kindness. Let us add a cheerful note to the depressing clamour around us. It costs so little, and gives so much pleasure. It does the heart good. It is so beautiful, and so pleasing to God. Pleasing to God, just fancy!

42

Mark xiv, 1–72; xv, 1–46

'The Passion of our Lord Jesus Christ. . . .'

Have you noticed how numerous are the crosses and crucifixes in the old houses and ancient towns, and how few instead there are in the new? In our grandfathers' houses there was never a room without a crucifix. You may object that, having become a convention, it no longer had the slightest effect, one way or the other, and there may be some truth in what you say—but today it is a desolation. It was very hard work getting the crucifix replaced in the schools, and the man who had it replaced[1] had no faith in it himself; he was doing this for the sake of the children, as even the philosophers agreed was permissible. The only places where the cross still stands undisturbed until now are the cemeteries, or at least our own cemeteries, and even there it soon falls to the ground, weakened and worn out, like our memory of the dead.

Let us admit that during these last two centuries the great mass of men have abandoned Christianity; they are barely now beginning to return, by slow stages and in small groups. Men have lost the Lord. Or, to be more precise, they have crucified him again. They have been more numerous and more determined than the men who crucified him on Calvary, and they have acted with more refined cruelty. Now they kill him

1. Mussolini.

in the hearts most dear to him, the hearts of humble people who live Christian lives, not for any worldly motive, not for their own advantage or as an intellectual experiment, not as a profession—men and women who live Christian lives because this is their only happiness. They kill him in the hearts of those who ask nothing of Christianity save the salvation of their souls, in the hearts of those who have no other earthly or heavenly wealth beyond the Christian hope.

In this truly holy week, which reminds us of the suffering and death of Jesus, let us reflect upon his suffering and death in humble hearts. Once the people of our countryside, our villages and townships, were an essentially Christian people. They thought and felt as Christians; 'Christian' was another name for a man: people said 'a good Christian', or 'a bad Christian', when they meant a good or bad man. Christianity was not then an activity, an ideology or culture, a profession or a programme. It was something intimately and profoundly grafted into our very nature, something felt more in some and less in others, so that we had at one extreme the saint and at the other the criminal. This feeling seemed to have become, as it were, part of us. The Christian festivals were really the festivals of the whole village or town. The finest buildings were the churches. The greatest wealth was used for the worship of God, and for the poor.

The political and social organizations were the latest and most reluctant to allow themselves to be permeated with Christianity. In fact, without formally opposing it they yielded none of their prerogatives, privileges and preponderance, justifying themselves with pretexts and legitimizing the lack of substance with an excess of outward show. These organizations in fact gave way only under the impact of violence. But the humble hearts, the simple souls, the majority of men in our lands, had imbibed the Christian doctrine in all sincerity. There was still much to do, but much had been accomplished.

Then in the world, in the same way as in our souls, there appeared, not a heresy to deny this or that part of Christian teaching, but an apostasy, all the more treacherous in that it

claimed to preserve all that was still alive in Christianity, and
to reject only what it considered was dead beyond recall. And
what was there chiefly that was dead beyond recall? There
was Jesus, the God Jesus. Therefore these new believers
paraded a great respect for Christianity as a phase in human
history, and considerable respect for Jesus the Man, but only
as man; there was an absolute denial of the divinity of Christ,
as of the personality of God and the immortality of the human
soul. Nothing much, as you see! And this denial was not
proclaimed in bitter and violent polemics, but expressed quite
calmly as if men were discussing some very obvious truths,
and an advance in knowledge that had come with the passing
of time—in fact, an improvement in Christianity itself: we
were to be Christians, but without Christ!

As long as this denial was the attitude of the so-called
educated classes, things went on much as before. Now that
it has come down to the humbler classes and has spread like
wildfire, we no longer feel ourselves to be men, with the
grandeurs and miseries of former times; we feel like herds
of animals or swarms of birds, bereft of all dignity, even, and
above all, in our suffering and death.

They killed Jesus, and we, as usual, ran away for fear they
would kill us too. The passion and death of Jesus continue
around us, perhaps also within us. And with the Man God
man dies too; we also die, with Jesus. We end unmourned,
done to death by hatred. Without leaving a record, like beasts.

43

Luke xxii, 1–17; xxiii, 1–53

'The Passion of our Lord Jesus Christ. . . .'

However hard it may be, we must sometimes face up to the blackest fact of our lives, the fact of our sin, and of the death we deal to Jesus in our own souls, and not on one occasion only.

It is not true that we do not think of this. Our lives are full of meditations, examinations of conscience, confessions and penances. There are so many of them that it is a matter for surprise, painful surprise, that we ever reach the point of sinning. Perhaps, falling into one of the Enemy's snares, we have, through furtive complicity with our lusts, created two separate compartments: on the one hand the life of prayer, and on the other the life of this world. In the one we can dissolve into tears, and in the other we become apostates. We never allow the two lives, lived in their separate compartments, to meet, in case they should come to blows. We smother sin with every sort of silencer, we muffle it with cautious excuses, at times we are even coy about it. Ah yes, we say, we are sinners, dreadful sinners. The Lord knows how deeply we offend him. We say this with a shame-faced air and a formal show of compunction.

We are very careful to keep the flame and the wood far

apart, and then we wonder why our fires do not light. We stuff our prayers with empty abstractions, set phrases, gestures that have lost their meaning for us, vague reflections and ceremonious invocations, with agitations and artificial fervour. We never let our prayer get to grips with the actualities of our lives, our real interests. We keep it at a distance, like a wild beast in a cage. With the excuse of not wishing to encourage distractions from the holy and sweet privacy of prayer we are most careful, when we pray, not to let our thoughts dwell on the course of our own affairs. The contrast would be too strident. Christianity must give us a fine outward appearance, a studied tranquillity of mind—that is all we ask for it; never must we let it loose, without lead or chain, in the garden of our soul. It must be held at a safe distance, lest it attack and bite. In this way, by acting like good Christians, we immunize ourselves against ever becoming good Christians.

Naturally, this method leads regularly to sin, and to grave sin. We kill Jesus, as his murderers did on Calvary, and although we do not put forward as our pretext the interests of God, as they did, at least we claim to continue to lead Christian lives. That this murder takes place in our secret conscience, without any outward visible sign, and without bringing us into bad repute, gives us impunity but does not excuse us—rather, it accuses us. Would we like to be pointed out as having been among those who crucified Jesus? Yet we are much guiltier than they were: the Lord could not pray for us to be forgiven, because we know very well what we are doing.

We know perfectly well that the money we put into our pockets costs the life of Jesus, in our soul. We know that we kill Jesus when we vie with each other and fight, striking slanderous and ambitious blows to raise ourselves higher and push our fellows further down. We know that Jesus dies in us if we linger over certain imaginings, or if we neglect to control our affections, if we consent to certain ambiguous relationships, if we give ourselves over to the pleasure of this world. We know that all we add to our glory is stolen from the glory of God—and so we drive Jesus out, Jesus who does not seek his own glory but his Father's.

When we read the Passion of Jesus we think of all he suffers in us, through our fault. It seems too horrible to be true, but it is true. We also, and more cruelly than his enemies, give him the traitor's kiss, we lie in wait for him at night to take him prisoner, we hand him over to our villainous passions, buffet him, crown him with thorns, spit upon him, scourge him without mercy, and drag him to the place of ignominy and death. We Christians offend him even when we are supposed to be doing him honour; this is when we do him honour, not for his own sake but for our own profit, to win glory for ourselves, and to further our own advancement.

While I write, and I am writing of Jesus, and of his suffering in us, my pen falters. I who write am like you who read, and you and I are like so many others, too many: murderers of Jesus, even in the act of remembering him. Have pity on us, Lord, we are such poor wretches!

44

'Now before the feast of the Passover, when Jesus knew that his hour had come to depart out of this world to the Father, having loved his own who were in the world, he loved them to the end.'

John xiii, 1

'... he loved them to the end'

He loved them to the end, to the extreme and bitter end. But have we ever measured the far-reaching significance of this expression? Words, even among us men, do not always lie—sometimes they really mean what they say. Most of us have met human beings who, in the way of goodness or evil, have gone through to the end, that cliff edge beyond which there is nothing but flight or a headlong fall. There are mothers who wear themselves out for their children; women who have loved till death, and in death; men who at the cost of their lives and possessions have served an ideal or a passion to the point of self-sacrifice. We must not judge men harshly, especially when we have set ourselves up to preach to them. Men, when they 'go all out,' can do wonders. But to do these, they must be men, and not merely this or that other thing which they are too often content to be; they must gather all their resources of strength, marshalling them all to battle, for a dream or a duty. Man, when he sets out to be great, knows he has greatness in him; and in order to be great,

146

he needs no special training; he does not even need to read and write; it is enough for him to be a man. Not for nothing did God love man, not for nothing does he still love him and think highly of him. It was he who created him, and he well knows what he is capable of achieving.

When from considering man, any man, we turn to consider humanity in our Lord, we at once see that the man in Jesus was not only the most highly endowed of men, not only without taint of sin and its consequences, but was himself the climax, the highest peak of humanity. We cannot conceive of a man who was more of a man than our Lord. Even in the humble form of a servant, as St Paul describes him, Jesus had in him all the greatest spiritual powers of the greatest men: Plato, Caesar, Homer, Virgil and so on. All the truth to which man can aspire was in Jesus, and all the goodness, strength, spiritual beauty and power. In the same way, he plumbed the depths of all that man can suffer.

Let us go further. The man in Jesus was united in unity of Person with the Word of God, himself God. What the humanity of Jesus must have received from his divinity in what was more a unity than a union, will always be lost for us in dazzling light—we shall never know, perhaps not even in Heaven. The last knowledge of God that we receive ends in adoration. What strength and what light the man who was in Jesus received from God who was in Jesus, the two natures being joined in the same Person, we can only surmise; the spiritual wealth of Jesus, already apparently without limits even within the bounds of humanity, is without any visible or invisible limits when we think of his divinity.

At this point, dear reader, I beg you to reflect with me upon the wonderful glimpse of the infinite that we find in these words of St John: 'he loved them to the end'. If our own capacity for love, when we extend it to the full, is so indescribably great, how incredibly great and inconceivable must be the capacity of Jesus, the Man God! If we, when we exert all our powers, cannot see the far horizons within our reach, how far must the reach of Jesus have extended, when he engaged his whole being?

Without any seeking after literary effect, and without that false air of piety which we too often assume as our mask on special occasions, but speaking with the objectivity with which we face the nude and crude reality of disease, or work, or passion—let us, you and I, reader, reflect a moment. Jesus has loved us, has loved you and loved me, to the end. We know well who Jesus is, we know what his love is like, we know what we, you and I, really are. How is it possible for us, for you and for me, to continue to live such wretched lives, as if Jesus did not exist, did not love us, had not loved us to the end? He is God, and he could not love us more than he does. What do we do about it, you and I?

45

John xviii, 1–40; xix, 1–42

'The Passion of our Lord Jesus Christ. . . .'

On this day Jesus died. He touched the depths of love and pain, he lived his last hour, breathed his last breath. At that moment we would not have known where to look: at the people around him, at the two thieves, crucified on either side of him, at our Lady and the mourning women, or at Jesus, worn out, exhausted, dripping blood, disfigured by wounds and fever, hanging on three nails. The sky must have been overcast, the light sinister. Above the hill the air was still, as if all life were about to cease. Death has its own greatness; there is something august and grand about it, an air of mystery. Indeed, it is a mystery. When any life flickers out, even in a flower or an insect, we are astonished and dismayed. And man's death has a certain majesty about it, something superhuman. Everything dies, and yet we are never resigned to this. It is hard to understand why a man should die. If he had to die, why was he born? If he was born, why should he die? All that a man has of beauty and grandeur seems made for something vaster than time and space. Thought is not confined in this way. How can so many cherished dreams, so many loves, so many thoughts, be lost for ever? And what abyss is immense enough to contain the wealth of humanity that passes from our sight?

149

On this day Jesus died, Jesus too died. For this reason alone we should love him most dearly. Death frightens and bewilders us: Jesus has taken us by the hand, as if we were children afraid of the dark, and has gone before us. His usual greeting was: Have no fear. He knew how many invincible fears pluck at our heart-strings. In the garden of olives he endured not only fear but terror. He felt not merely doubt but revulsion, the bitterest revulsion. He drained the chalice of our bewilderment and dismay to the dregs. He had not wished to put his lips to it, but he drank it all.

On this day Jesus died. We killed him. It is no use trying to evade this, no use looking for alibis. We all, with no exception, are responsible for his death. Our right place is not with the Maries beneath the Cross; it is with those who crucified him. Today, of all days, we ought to read this truth in one another's eyes—this unimaginable crime. It was we who killed him.

On this day Jesus died. And as if it were not enough to have killed him once, we were to kill him again, every time we sinned. We were to repeat the insults and the stripes, every kind of infamy, and death. The most inane fancy, the dirtiest jest, would be enough to induce us to kill Jesus again.

On this day Jesus died. He was dying for men, and there would be some who would mock at his death, spurn him, and by so doing lose their immortal souls. It seems impossible that such an incredible thing could be true, that every one of us can render the death of Jesus of no avail for himself; every one of us can condemn himself, in spite of Jesus and his Blood, his love and death.

On this day Jesus died. And by dying he reopened to us the Heavens, restored us to our Father, gave us back our eternal home, and made us once more children of God, brothers to him, Jesus, and brothers to each other. In dying he conquered death, disarmed sin and unsealed the fountain of grace; he was, as it were, re-creating us. Today we are reborn as children of God. He died and we were born. We were born of his Heart, drained of blood, pierced through with the point of a lance.

O Lord, we cannot even lift our eyes to you on the Cross.

We cannot even stand with your Mother beneath it. It is true! we killed you, and perhaps we have killed you again. But, Lord, do not think of this. Think that you died for us, for us all, for every one of us. Do not let me perish—do not let one soul perish, not one single soul. We cannot bear to think, O Jesus, how greatly you loved us and how meagre is our love for you.

46

'Now after the sabbath, toward the dawn of the first day of the week, Mary Magdalene and the other Mary went to see the sepulchre. And behold, there was a great earthquake; for an angel of the Lord descended from Heaven and came and rolled back the stone and sat upon it. His appearance was like lightning, and his raiment white as snow. And for fear of him the guards trembled and became like dead men. But the angel said to the women, "Do not be afraid; for I know that you seek Jesus who was crucified. He is not here; for he has risen, as he said."'

Matthew xxviii, 1–7

'His appearance was like lightning, and his raiment white as snow'

The brightest gleam we know, that of a flash of lightning, and the most dazzling whiteness, that of snow, had already been seen in the transfiguration, appearing and disappearing; now they shone once more on the day of resurrection, and they shine for ever. Just two images, two appearances, but full of awful meaning. Flame in its most terrifying form, a flash of lightning followed by a mysterious clap of thunder, and snow of utter whiteness, a whiteness that seems not so much a reflection as a blinding birth of light, offer us a brief glimpse of what our glorified bodies will be like, after the example and through the merit of the Body of our Lord.

152

We know the weakness and the suffering of our body, but we do not try to know its mystery, which is much greater than its weakness. On the one hand it is part of the life of all creation, and lived like an animal or like a flower; on the other hand, through its intelligence and will it is part of the life of its Creator. It is like the bridge between matter and spirit, like the last screen between God and material creation.

All the varied beauties of the created universe are in some way expressed and repeated in the body. A sunlit leaf, the flight of a bird, a light in someone's eyes, colour fading from twilit waters, all that is most gentle and delicate is reflected also in man. And we need not speak of all the rest, which is grandiose: his nutrition and respiration, the circulation of his blood, his locomotion and reproduction, are like so many created worlds which it has taken us centuries to discover, and to reveal whose secrets we shall need many centuries more, if indeed we ever succeed.

Whereas in the world of matter great powers of perception and application are not so necessary to understand the marvels of our bodies, to understand the spiritual world we must have continual recourse to meditation. The understanding and the will form part, not of the body but of the soul, of which they are the supreme faculties. This is quite true, but it is also true that they reside with the soul in the body, and the body is not a residence for occasional use, or for a brief stay, but is their natural, continual and eternal home. At the moment of death the soul is separated from the body, but it will not find complete happiness, even in Paradise, until it has recovered its own body with the resurrection of the dead. The understanding and the will, although essentially spiritual faculties, and, unlike the sensitive faculties, not dependent on a bodily organ, nevertheless live in the body as in their proper sphere. And this is the other marvel, the other order of indescribable marvels with regard to which our bodies are at the same time the spectators, the actors, and the theatre.

How beautiful it is to see the sea awakening at dawn, to rest on the verge of a forest, to hear a storm raging while one is warmly and safely in bed, or to admire from a high terrace the summer sky strewn with stars! But all this strikes us as beautiful because it not only arouses sensations, as if we were merely animal, or had merely vital functions like a plant, but suggests feelings which are largely composed of thought and love. The awareness of our essence, which is not so much physical as spiritual, confers on us a dignity that makes the poorest of men of greater worth than the grandest and most impressive natural scenery, so that the voice of a weeping child is in a certain sense more powerful than the roar of the sea, the crash of thunder, or the howling of the wind in a mountain ravine. Many have mocked at the majesty of man— yes, majesty is the right word—pointing out his absurdities and insufficiencies. But it remains a fact that God so loved man, and a man's body, that he became a man, and took our body for his own.

He did not take it as he found it, soiled with sin, a dismal lair for unleashed instincts and maddened lusts. He took it immaculate and holy from his holy and immaculate Mother, and bore it with joy and glory, with all its grief and suffering. He bore it to the Cross, and on this day when he broke out from the sepulchre, it is as if he said to us: Did I not tell you to have no fear? This is my body, and your body. Yes, yours, the body of every one of you, of every one who does not refuse it. You now see in what purity of substance, and what radiance of light the body of man, once so radiant as it left the Father's hands, today issues from the cleansing flow of my blood, the fire of my love, the power of my new covenant.

47

*'And when the Sabbath was past, Mary Magdalene, and
Mary the mother of Jesus, and Salome, brought spices, so
that they might go and anoint him. And very early on the
first day of the week they went to the tomb when the sun had
risen. And they were saying to one another, "Who will roll
away the stone for us from the door of the tomb?" And looking up, they saw that the stone was rolled back; for it was
very large. And entering the tomb, they saw a young man
sitting on the right side, dressed in a white robe; and they
were amazed. And he said to them, "Do not be amazed; you
seek Jesus of Nazareth, who was crucified. He has risen, he is
not here . . ." '*

Mark xvi, 1–6

'You seek Jesus of Nazareth, who was crucified.
He has risen, he is not here'

The Angel's words would be a fitting reply to those who
look for Jesus, but without greatly desiring to find him; or to
those who seek him as a man, and only as a man. It is a fit
reply to the learned without faith, as also to the ignorant without faith, and to all who persist in telling the story of
Christianity, the story of the world, the story of society, the
story of every conceivable thing that has a story, and then,
when they come to Jesus, accept him as a man and reject
him as a God. Let us leave them to look for him, leave them

to their hopeless search, if they refuse to join us—let them go on raking among the tombs, if they will not come away.

We believe, we know, I would even say we feel, that Jesus, crucified for but a few hours, has risen for eternity. It is quite useless to look for him among the dead; he is no longer there, as the Angel said, and as we all, every one of us, may say. He has risen again. And in the natural history of mankind there is room for the dead, but no room for those who have risen again.

In fact, the Christian's overflowing joy derives from this infringement, if we may so call it, of the rules of history, understood as natural history, this resurrection of the Lord. St Paul understood very well the meaning of the resurrection. It is the ultimate proof that we are not imprisoned in the world of matter, bound hand and foot, nor are we the prisoners of sin or death. Someone has broken these chains, and broken them for all peoples and all ages. Sin is no longer unconquered and unconquerable. Death is not the final disaster. The world can no longer frighten us with its pleasures, and its terrors: it has been overcome. The enemy may prowl about like a lion, but a new born baby, fresh from the waters of baptism, is enough to terrify him and put him to flight.

Let us remember, Christians, the meaning of the resurrection of Christ. With him mankind rose again. With him we were reborn to eternal life. Because of him no one is any longer a child of wrath, or a slave, chained to the devil and damnation. Because of him death is a passage, not an arrival; it is a sorrow, not a condemnation, a trial, not a vengeance.

.   .   .   .   .

Now that Jesus has risen again we recover possession of our poor bodies, restored in the waters of repentance; we recover possession of the created universe; we recover possession of our brother men and of God our Father. Life has acquired a sense, a significance and a direction. Everything we do has eternal value. Death has been overcome, and with it all that was ephemeral; all that is eternal now reigns and triumphs in our hearts. Even suffering is changed and transformed into a means of ascension, a purification and a redemption. St Paul heard the groans of the world of nature, which also brings forth in pain, and is bound to death and destruction: he knew well in what perfection nature too had issued from the hands of God. St Peter could not renounce the hope that our Saviour would one day lay his sacred, wounded hands on nature, and heal her too: we do not know what the new Heavens and the new earth will be like, but we know that they will be.

Meanwhile, men's hearts are renewed, their souls redeemed. The resurrection morning is the morning of the Earthly Paradise regained: men re-enter it, following Jesus, the new Adam, who rose again.

48

'That very day two of them were going to a village named Emmaus, about seven miles from Jerusalem, and talking with each other about all these things that had happened. While they were talking and discussing together, Jesus himself drew near and went with them. But their eyes were kept from recognizing him. . . . So they drew near to the village to which they were going. He appeared to be going further, but they constrained him, saying, "Stay with us, for it is toward evening and the day is far spent." So he went in to stay with them. When he was at table with them, he took the bread and blessed, and broke it, and gave it to them. And their eyes were opened and they recognized him; and he vanished out of their sight.'

Luke xxiv, 13–31

'And he vanished out of their sight'

The two disciples were overjoyed. They had spent whole days in close companionship with Jesus, but they had never felt as they did now, with a strange and powerful excitement in their hearts. They could not remember ever having been so happy. If there is such a thing as bliss, they thought, we are about to experience it. The Apostles who were present at the transfiguration, when Peter said he wished to set up three tents and stay for ever on that hill-top, must have felt the same. It was like a glimpse of eternal life—an anticipa-

tion, a foretaste and a pledge, as much for the Apostles on
Mount Tabor, as for the disciples at Emmaus.

These gleams of eternity are but momentary—lasting no
longer on this earth than a solitary flash of lightning in the
night. He vanished out of their sight. Just at the best moment
of all, when the disciples thought they were about to enjoy
the happiness they saw shining before them, Jesus appeared
and disappeared in the same moment. They saw him, and he
was gone. If they had had no other proof of his identity they
would have known him by the sense of unquenchable joy
springing up in their hearts. Even when he goes away, Jesus
does not leave us disenchanted and deluded; he leaves us with
our hearts still on fire. St John of the Cross, in one of those
other-worldly poems in which he describes the love the Son
of God has for his creatures, expresses this state of mind: 'I
ran after you, crying out; you had gone!' The disciples at
Emmaus must have run after Jesus in the same way, but in
vain. He was no longer to be seen on our roads, could no
longer be pursued and overtaken. So they ran to their brothers
in the faith. When we feel the presence of Jesus we at once
wish to rejoin our brothers. The love that rises to the Father
from our hearts falls back to us as love for our neighbour.
The saints most highly endowed with the graces of prayer
are always those who felt most keenly love for their neighbour.
Communion of life with the Father—but a real communion,
not just as we use the word—brings with it in equal measure
a communion of life with our brothers.

We too, unless we are among those unhappy creatures
whose prayers are a mere formality, or a habitual exercise,
may at times feel the presence of Jesus. We do not mean in
apparitions, visions or other supernatural ways proper to the
saints and not to all, or even most, of them. The meeting we
speak of consists in a very vivid and delightful sense of his
presence; a presence not visible or tangible, not apparent to
our senses, and yet mysteriously made known to our hearts.
Sometimes our prayer, because of some unusual purity of
heart and through the grace of God, is aware of a light other
than that of the sun, and sees with eyes other than those of our

body. We go on praying for a while, but it is as if time and space no longer existed. We feel, but in an incomparably greater and more intense way, as we do when we are lost in thought: that is, to all intents and purposes we lose consciousness of the material and bodily conditions of our life.

These are the oases of sweet and most refreshing prayer, in the desert of our lives. We go on day after day, thirsty and covered with the dust of the road, under the blinding and scorching sun, in the midst of perils and fatigues; and at last we find an hour of divine refreshment. Let us thank the Lord for it, and remember that it is his custom to reveal himself, and give himself, even more fully when he appears to be most closely veiled: in the sacrament of bread and wine, the sacrament of death and life, in the breaking of bread. And let us remember too that not only does he reveal himself to us when he breaks the divine bread of his body, but also when we break a little wheaten loaf and share it with our poorer brothers. How blessed we should be if we could, in the same way, break and share with them the whole of our life!

49

'... Then they told what had happened on the road, and how he was known to them in the breaking of the bread. As they were saying this, Jesus himself stood among them, and said to them, "Peace to you." But they were startled and frightened, and supposed that they saw a spirit. And he said to them, "Why are you troubled, and why do questionings arise in your hearts? See my hands and my feet, that it is I myself; handle me, and see; for a spirit has not flesh and bones as you see that I have!"'

Luke xxiv, 35–9

'... it is I myself'

Every morning, as if at some bugle call that you alone can hear, you prepare for the day's march; you get up, cleanse yourself from the shadows and stains of sleep, dress, open your window and see the sun. As you cross your threshold and set out on your daily road, remember his words: It is I myself. I have created for you the black night and the dawn; I have given you your body and its repose, your sleep and re-awakening, your eyes and your light, your feet and your road. I myself have done this.

When, after leaving your house, you enter, as I would like to hope you do, some church to visit me in the sacrament of my love and yours, of my death and your life, and when you kneel at one of the pews, in line with a few other friends of mine, when you listen to the Mass and make your communion, there is no need for me to tell you that it is I whom you visit, whom you receive, whom you take away. But think how many there are who know that I am here, present in the sacrament, and yet spare no thought for me! No one comes to find me here, and yet I myself am present in this empty church.

When you reach your place of work, physical labour, clerical duties or business, you do this and that; and all you do is done for others, and for you there remains but the slender margin of a salary or wage. Remember I am there. Yes, I myself am working with you, I have given you your strength and skill; I am in all those for whom you work; I myself am there. I work with you and you work for me. I am present with you.

When you are dealing with a superior, I am there in him, and when you are dealing with an inferior I am there in him too. I am in every one of you, and you are all equal; all your superiorities and inferiorities merely mean a greater or lesser service, that is all. The insolence with which you regard a superior wounds me; the scorn with which you treat an inferior is a blow to me. In every one of you I myself am there.

When in the midst of your toil you see that all is going very well or (and this happens more frequently) all is going very badly, do not rejoice too much, or be too downcast. What matters is that you have done your best. You are not working for success or fortune—you are working for me, and nothing escapes my watchful eye. Spend yourself to the full extent of your powers, and have no fear: I am your true reward, your true joy. I myself am with you.

When temptation (there are thousands of temptations but all have only one aim, to make you abandon me) when temptation begins to entice you or, changing its tactics, tries to terrify you, do not be afraid. You think you are sinking; you are on the point of sinking—but if you call to me I am by your side. I myself am here.

When disaster falls upon you and sweeps away, like withered stalks, your time-tables, your plans, your legitimate hopes and perhaps even the whole order of your life, confining you to bed, racked with suffering and despair, you may think that those who love you can do nothing more for you, and that God, who could help you, has no love for you, then, and especially then, remember I am with you. Between the garden of olives and the Cross I too was in dire straits. I too know that wilderness without a single voice, the wilderness of death. I too know how unbearable is the Cross, and even more unbearable our duty to bear it; but I have carried it for you and I will always help you to carry yours. Everything deserts you, everything passes away—but I do not desert you, or pass away. I myself am with you.

I am the only begotten Son of God, and your elder brother. I am your source and your outpouring, your setting out, your road, and your arrival. I myself am with you. I am the presence of the Father with you, and your presence with him. I am he whom you most cruelly wronged; I am he who most dearly loved you. I myself am at the beginning of time, in the midst of time and at the end. I am in your brother as I am in you. You flee from me in all directions but you cannot elude me. You find me before you on every road. If you run away from my love you incur my wrath. Look at me, look at me well, unhappy man: I myself am here.

50

'Just as day was breaking, Jesus stood on the beach; yet the disciples did not know that it was Jesus. Jesus said to them, "Children, have you any fish?" They answered him, "No." He said to them, "Cast the net on the right side of the boat, and you will find some." So they cast it, and now they were not able to haul it in, for the quantity of fish. That disciple whom Jesus loved said to Peter, "It is the Lord!" When Simon Peter heard that it was the Lord, he put on his clothes, for he was stripped for work, and sprang into the sea.'

John xxi, 4–7

'It is the Lord'

This episode is continually repeated in the history of the Church and in the history of our souls. We often, too often, in fact, lose sight of the Lord, and then some good soul reminds us of him, or perhaps a noble sentiment, a good book, or a fortunate encounter helps us to remember him. It is the Lord, we are told. And we tremble, as if he were a spirit, or a ghost.

In the thick of the most dreadful conflicts suffered by the Church in two thousand years of life it has seemed more than once as if the pilot of the divine boat had been overcome by the darkness of night, and by fatigue. The saints have cried out to him: It is the Lord. The pilot has not only ceased to

tremble for his boat, but has cast himself into the water, with
holy daring, to go to meet the Lord.

Under the stress of a temptation or an ordeal our intelligence loses its grip, we no longer know where we are, what we
are doing, what is to be done, or how. If only our other spiritual faculties would hold their peace, but no, they are like so
many furies unleashed. It is a fearful pandemonium, a bitter
agitation of mind. In these circumstances the voice of a friend
may show us where Jesus is. He may suggest to us a good
book, or a good deed.

I once knew a man who, when he felt exhausted with the
conflict and the temptation, used to go to visit someone either
gravely ill or desperately poor. He said it was only by doing
this that he could find the Lord, who seemed to elude him
everywhere else. And his conflicts and temptations were by
no means inspired by base desires (as we are generally so
ready to believe, as if no other sins existed); they were, let us
say with a tinge of irony, superior battles and temptations.
This friend of mine was exceptionally gifted, and suffered
from fits of giddy and overpowering vanity. He told me
frankly that, after an exhibition of his powers, he had the
impression that the whole of creation had gathered around
to applaud him. He was no vain fool, no ridiculous megalo-
maniac; undoubtedly he had one gift, but it was one only,
which was immeasurably and incomparably great. In appearance he was modesty personified, because he scrupulous-
ly avoided exhibitionism and the admiration of the crowds.
But in his soul, he told me, there was always a sort of Vanity
Fair, with every sort of vanity on show. At times his soul was
totally darkened by this. Then he would escape to visit someone dying of cancer, or an almost unapproachable pauper.
He used to say laughingly that a meek and mild pauper was
of no use to him; he needed an aggressive and insolent type.
In fact, he seemed to have a flair for discovering the most
ferocious specimens, and sometimes I was horrified to see
him coming home arm in arm with one of these; I felt as if
he had come back with a rattlesnake on a lead.

He was an odd fellow, but he was quite right: pain and

poverty showed him the presence of the Lord. We know that Jesus had a special love for the poor and the suffering, as great as the love he had for John. It is indeed the humble who remind us of Jesus, the humblest people, the humblest things. It is not by chance that the beggar appeals to us 'for the love of God', whereas no one with any worldly position to consider would dare to make use of his name when offering us work, or a collaboration, or a business deal. It is not by chance that when we talk to sick men the conversation naturally turns to the subject of God, whereas this name could never crop up in the middle of a Lucullian banquet, a hard-fought game, or an evening's amusement. We have reached the point when the thought of God and his presence makes us feel melancholy—while those who lack everything, even health, find company and comfort in thinking of him. It naturally follows that the poor and the suffering have a special instinct for recognizing Jesus and revealing his presence.

We must also remember that the Lord is really more frequently present where there is someone in distress. However hard he may be to find, he is very rarely absent from a sick man's room, or a poor man's house. He is in the sacraments and teaching of his Church, he is in the hospitals, prisons and shelters; he is with all who suffer.

51

'But Mary stood weeping outside the tomb, and as she wept she stooped to look into the tomb; and she saw two angels in white, sitting where the body of Jesus had lain, one at the head and one at the feet. They said to her, "Woman, why are you weeping?" She said to them, "Because they have taken away my Lord, and I do not know where they have laid him." Saying this, she turned round and saw Jesus standing, but she did not know that it was Jesus. Jesus said to her, "Woman, why are you weeping? Whom do you seek?" Supposing him to be the gardener, she said to him, "Sir, if you have carried him away, tell me where you have laid him, and I will take him away." '

John xx, 11–15

'I will take him away'

How beautiful are these words of Mary's, and how grand her intention, so far beyond her strength! She was going to take him away, from wherever they had carried him. She had the courage to rescue that sacred corpse from any foe. It is the cry of the Crusaders, the gesture of St Clare of Assisi when she saved the Blessed Sacrament, it is the attitude of all who are ready to sacrifice their lives for what they love. Perhaps Mary Magdalen owes her supreme privilege of being the first to see the risen Christ to the fact that she was the first to go to look for him. She may have spent the night watching, like the Bride in the Song of Solomon, among the shadows and the dews of dawn. One day St Ambrose was to link together the words of the Song of Songs and the example of Mary Magdalen, and apply them to every loving soul who goes in search of Jesus. And the words of St Ambrose will live for ever and form one of the noblest and most tender commentaries on prayer and virginity.

But we must remember that Mary Magdalen had been a sinner. She is in the great tradition of Peter, who cannot find words to convince Jesus how much he loves him, and of St Paul, who never knew the satisfaction of feeling that he had sufficiently preached and interpreted him; in the great tradition of St Augustine and of all penitent souls. The example of this wonderful woman shows us that sin itself, when it is forgiven, becomes an irresistible motive for love. When the saints set out to find Jesus, their starting point was always their sorrow for the sins they had committed.

It is only we who are ashamed, literally ashamed, to speak of our sins, and if we do speak of them, it is in very vague and generic terms. We should not dream of presenting ourselves under our first and most authentic title, that of sinners. And not sinners in the abstract, but sinners guilty of these and those particular sins. Yet, this is the only description that suits us down to the ground, and the only one we deserve.

We must resign ourselves to the thought that without an honest confession of our sin, and a hard and effective penance, we shall never feel a love for God worthy of the name. As long as we leave sin in the background it will be free to lay waste the garden of our soul. Until we challenge it resolutely, calling it aloud by its name, sin will not loosen its grip on us. Mary Magdalen understood that she could not become another creature until she had stopped being the creature she was. When St Paul speaks of sin and grace he speaks very plainly of a death and a resurrection.

.   .   .   .   .

How can we claim to love Jesus unless we first resolve to

confess our sin? To confess it, judge it, condemn it and put it to death? We cannot imagine a Christian life cheerfully and nonchalantly balanced between sin and forgiveness. It would be a strident abuse of forgiveness, it would mean drawing it into complicity with frailty and iniquity. The ease with which we obtain sacramental forgiveness must not induce us to confuse the mercy of God with a sort of connivance in our sin. The example of Mary Magdalen must remind us that sin does not stand in the way of a great love for the Lord, provided only that sin be fully acknowledged, expiated and mourned.

By ourselves we should not be capable of slaying that monster, sin. Beside us and for us fights the grace of God, but even with all this grace the battle is still very hard fought, very dangerous, and may even be fatal. O my friends, if we want to live to see the radiance of a dawn like this Resurrection morning, we must first endure the suffering and death of Jesus. Let us bear this in mind, and then we shall no longer be such poor cowards, causing Jesus so much grief and shame.

52

'Now the eleven disciples went to Galilee, to the mountain to which Jesus had directed them. And when they saw him they worshipped him; but some doubted. And Jesus came and said to them, "All authority in Heaven and on earth has been given to me. Go therefore and make disciples of all nations, baptizing them in the name of the Father, and of the Son and of the Holy Ghost, teaching them to observe all that I have commanded you; and lo, I am with you always, to the close of the age." '

Matthew xxviii, 16–20

'... but some doubted'

Not only is there always some doubter among us, but within us too there is always some contradiction: there is no truth which does not contain a shade and suspicion of the contrary, and no good deed which from some point of view and in a certain sense cannot be bad. We must not let a little thing like this make us despair, but it is certainly disquieting. The more we study, the greater seems the darkness on our path; the better we are the more clearly we see all sorts of stains on our soul. Among really intelligent people we shall never find an intellectual braggart, or one who is always displaying his brains in the shop window; the intellect has its own reserve which rarely fails it: even a man like Dante Alighieri, who from a distance seems boldness personified, cannot have made a great impression when seen in flesh and blood, if four or five nobodies of his city and day could so easily turn him out, and enjoy money, honours and success while he remained exiled and unhappy. And goodness is even more shy than intelligence, being much more modest and, when it is real goodness, never sure of itself.

Let us not lose heart then, if doubt is for ever raising its head and temptation assailing us on all sides. Our life is warfare, not peace; it is a journey, not a halt.

It would, however, be unpardonable foolishness, and might be a cause of danger, if we were to dwell too long on doubts and temptations. They exist, but other things exist too, and they never represent the greater and the better part of ourselves. They exist, but truth is greater, and goodness is more beautiful. They exist, but they are here to serve, not to dominate. If a man were to pay too much attention to them and concentrate all his spiritual energies upon them, he would be behaving like one who cannot open his mouth without slandering his neighbour. It may well be that our neighbour is full of faults, but he has good qualities too, although we only speak of his defects. A hunchback may have a fine voice, a wonderful soul, a brilliant brain; for us he is simply a hunchback. All this is really more our stupidity than our malice.

Life, around us and within us, taken as a whole, has things in it which are neither true nor good, but in its essence it is true and good. Even original sin has not fundamentally warped our nature, which is the work of God, a work which has its limitations like all created things, but is good. God alone is infinite goodness, essential truth.

These reflections may seem very trite, and certainly they are not original. But we always forget these facts when we deal with our souls. We are ready to hand over a precious store of truth at the least sign of doubt, especially when we are tempted. We are ready to cast overboard months of prayer and penitence, at the request of the most foolish and insidious temptation. We scream like geese pursued when the sky of our soul darkens with clouds; when the vessel of our conscience finds herself battling with contrary winds we are in despair.

There is in us, and there always will be, something to rob us of sound sleep at night; if there were nothing else there would be our own mortality, which means that we may die from one moment to another. But even this, which is undoubtedly a grim thought, may have its own uses: it keeps us from being proud or vain.

And if ever we feel impelled to show our fellows how good we are, how clever and handsome, we must murmur in each other's ears: Careful! not only God but your fellow men also know how little you have of goodness in you, what a meagre store of brain or beauty. Indeed, God in his justice sees both good and evil; men see only the evil, and when they see you preening yourself they will say that you are not only ugly but a fool.

53

'*Mary Magdalen . . . ran, and went to Simon Peter and the other disciple, the one whom Jesus loved, and said to them, "They have taken the Lord out of the tomb, and we do not know where they have laid him." Peter then came out with the other disciple, and they went toward the tomb. They both ran, but the other disciple outran Peter and reached the tomb first; and stooping to look in, he saw the linen cloths lying there, but he did not go in. Then Simon Peter came, following him, and went into the tomb; he saw the linen cloths lying, and the napkin, which had been on his head, not lying with the linen cloths but rolled up in a place by itself. Then the other disciple, who reached the tomb first, also went in, and he saw and believed. . . .*'

John xx, 1–8

'. . . the other disciple'

My patient reader, we have now met fifty-three times, for these frank and confidential talks. This is the last time, and as I take my leave of you I feel impelled to beg your pardon. You must not think that this is a great virtue on my part, or a mere formality; it is simply that I would like to think I had given you no satisfaction at all apart from the salutary satisfaction of remorse; but I understand that it cannot have worked out like that, and that I must have given you a great deal of satisfaction, and not much of it was good for you. I would like to think I had spoken not too unworthily of the Lord, who was the third party to all our conversations, and for whom alone I wrote and you read; but I know well that this too is rarely achieved, so rarely that he is greatly blessed who succeeds.

At times you may have thought I was being clever, and at other times you may have thought me a fool. You should not have been thinking of me at all. I tell you this, and you can believe me, because I too was tempted, as I wrote, by no other desire than that of avoiding your displeasure and provoking your applause. So perhaps we have each been unable to see the wood for the trees. We should have been meditating on the real subject of my discourse, but instead you were thinking of me, the writer, and I was thinking of you, the reader. For my part I was trying to say things in such a way as to make you admire me, while you, in your turn, were trying to read into my words something that would prevent you from admiring me, especially if you know me personally, and, as we say, like a brother. In the natural order of things writer and reader would seem to have been made to get on well together, but it does not seem to be like that because usually the writer has little respect for his reader, regarding him as a fisherman regards a sprat. In his turn the reader, when he buys a book, is convinced that he has bought the author too, with all his relations to the fourth generation, forbears and descendants, and speaks with horrifying freedom and familiarity—I mean when he speaks, not of the book but of the author, his family, his relatives, his province, etc., etc. Mere foibles, of course, but we are stuffed full of them!

I have really tried to do nothing else, in these homely five-minute chats, but point out these weaknesses of ours. I have merely tried to hollow out a little course for the water of divine grace, digging a furrow here and there to make a channel for it, especially where the soil was most parched and untilled. I have tried to lift certain themes out of the sphere of rhetoric and platitudes, and let them circulate a little in the open air and among living things. When we are in a devout mood we are as demure as cooing doves, but in any other mood we are more awkward and quarrelsome than peevish hens. I wanted, above all, to recapture the frequent, living, close companionship of Jesus. At times we pray to him in such a way as to ensure that we remain as far away from him as possible; and we achieve the diabolical result of reducing to a sort of new paganism the revelation of the Father, the incarnation of the Son and the descent of the Holy Spirit.

We would do anything rather than recognize one another as brothers, essentially brothers, brothers and nothing else, all of us, including the noblest and meanest of men. I wished to introduce a little freshness and spontaneity into subjects which we confuse by alternately proclaiming and concealing, and which we never treat in a practical matter-of-fact way, but always with a 'clerical accent', a lofty and remote manner, and wide, meaningless gestures and grimaces.

And it is good to leave one another in the company of Peter and John on this miraculous morning.

John, who was younger and whose conscience was less laden than Peter's, arrived first. Peter must have been already somewhat advanced in years, and then, we know what he had been through. Some days were to go by before the Lord spoke to him again about that, and when he did there were bitter tears. John waited for Peter. They were fond of each other. Both had been called to a supreme destiny. You and I are two puny little Christians, but we too want to run ahead. If you get there first wait for me—let us help each other along this most beautiful of all roads, which will lead us to the Lord. I am not Peter, any more than you, perhaps, are John, but even if we had been the only people in the world, the Lord would have died for us two. Yes, he would have died for just the two of us. It is unbelievable but true: for me and for you he would have died. He did die. Let us stay together then, and love one another. Let us help one another to love Jesus. The rest is but vanity and sin.